**Inquiries should be addressed to:**
Victory Church
2650 Audubon Rd
Audubon, PA 19403
INVITEYOURNEIGHBOR.COM

*Invite Your Neighbor* may be purchased in bulk for educational, church, business, fundraising, or promotinal use. Please visit InviteYourNeighbor.com/bulk for bulk order details.

Scriptures taken from the Holy Bible, New International Version®, NIV®. Copyright © 1973, 1978, 1984, 2011 by Biblica, Inc.™ Used by permission of Zondervan. All rights reserved worldwide. Zondervan.com The "NIV" and "New International Version" are trademarks registered in the United States Patent and Trademark Office by Biblica, Inc.™

Scripture quotations marked NLT are taken from the Holy Bible. New Living Translation. © 1996, 2004, 2015 by Tyndale House Foundation. Used by permission of Tyndale House Publishers, Inc., Carol Stream, Illinois 60188. All rights reserved.

Scriptures marked ESV are from the ESV® Bible (The Holy Bible, English Standard Version®). Copyright © 2001 by Crossway, a publishing ministry of Good News Publishers. Used by permission. All rights reserved.

Italics in Scripture quotations reflect the author's added emphasis.

## Library of Congress Cataloging-in-Publication Data

Names: Crenshaw, Ed, author.
Title: Invite your neighbor : change the world / Ed Crenshaw.
Description: First Edition. | Audubon, Pennsylvania : Victory Church, 2021.
Identifiers: LCCN 2021909729 | ISBN 9780578916125
Subjects: LCSH: Love–Religious Aspects–Christianity. | Neighborliness–Religious Aspects–Christianity. | Christian Leadership. | Church Renewal–Christianity. | Spirituality–Christianity.

Cover and interior design: Steve Thurston
Author photo: Josiah Blizzard
Images used under license from Shutterstock.

Printed in the United States of America at ITP of USA, Elizabethtown, PA.
2021 Paperback Limited Edition

ISBN: 978-0-578-91612-5

21  22  23  24  25  26  27     10  9  8  7  6  5  4  3  2  1

# INVITE YOUR NEIGHBOR

## CHANGE THE WORLD

ED CRENSHAW

# INVITE YOUR NEIGHBOR

## GROUP SESSION 1

### CREATED TO MAKE A DIFFERENCE

You were created to make a difference. It's incredible that Jesus looked out over the desperate crowds that flocked around him and declared, "You are the salt of the earth. You are the light of the world." Jesus' words are true of you, as one of his followers, too. You have a preserving influence on a decaying world. You bring light into the darkness. God has a wonderful plan for your life, and a major part of that plan is your spiritual influence on the people in your world. Over the next six weeks, we will be stepping into this plan more fully. *Jesus came to bring you abundant life, and that means a fruitful life for God's glory and the blessing of others. You will enter into greater joy for yourself, too, as you take steps toward fulfilling God's plan for your life.*

If you have never been intentional about making a spiritual impact or sharing your faith, this could sound a little intimidating. Jesus gave us a simple way, however, to make an impact on others that would lead them to glorify God. It's such a simple way that we can easily overlook it, but if we will become intentional, and if we do it with other followers of Jesus, we will feel less intimidated and we will multiply our influence for good. You will bless both neighbors who are on the margins of your life, and neighbors who are in your everyday life. You will be a force for healing and reconciliation.

**You will be a force for healing and reconciliation.**

Our approach for this effort centers on Jesus' words in Matthew 5:16:

> *In the same way, let your light shine before others, that they may see your good deeds and glorify your Father in heaven.*

Jesus is very clear here: Our good deeds when seen by others will lead them to glorify God. It's as simple as that. If we are to take Jesus at his word— and we should—we can expect people to grow closer to God when they see what we do to serve people in need. So, what's the problem?

## THE PROBLEM: HOW DO PEOPLE IN OUR EVERYDAY LIVES SEE OUR GOOD DEEDS?

The church I pastor has put lots of effort into doing good deeds. We have worked with other churches in the region to serve the needs of our community. The people we have served directly have been blessed. Most of the good deeds done through church outreaches have served people on the margins of our lives and sometimes on the margins of society. That's great. *The question is, how does this help our church members' influence their friends, family, coworkers, and classmates, what I call our everyday neighbors, for Jesus?* Surely we should be impacting our everyday world for Jesus. How are these everyday neighbors going to see the good deeds we are doing for the people who need our good deeds the most?

## THE SOLUTION: INVITE OUR EVERYDAY NEIGHBORS TO SERVE WITH US

The solution is to invite our everyday neighbors, the people in our everyday world, to serve alongside us when we go out to serve as a church. What better way to serve a hurting world than to do so with our church family? What better way for our everyday neighbors to see the church in action than to invite them to serve with us? And if what Jesus says is true—and we can count on him for truth—these everyday neighbors will see Jesus' light and glorify our Father. Many of us have been inviting these everyday neighbors to worship with us for years, sometimes with discouraging results. Here's an important reality about the people around us, whom we want to influence for Jesus: Some people are ready to serve with us before they are ready to worship with us.

> Some people are ready to serve with us before they are ready to worship with us.

Besides committing to working through this study together, we are asking you to do just two things:

1. **Commit to a service project on your church's or group's day of service.**
2. **Invite someone who is not yet a follower of Jesus to serve with you.**

That's it. It's very simple. I know there is much more to evangelism than this, but we are going to take Jesus at his word regarding Matthew 5:16.

## WHY DO THIS STUDY? WE MUST BE SPIRITUALLY ENGAGED.

Since this is such a simple concept, why do we need to do a study? The study is vital because, while the concept is simple, and the two major commitments are rather easy, the dynamics we are putting into action are manifold. We aren't going to complicate things, but the more we understand these dynamics, the more effective we will be. We need to understand the "why" behind our approach, primarily because this is not just a formula. This effort is not just a series of steps that work in a mechanical way. *For us to produce spiritual fruit, our hearts must be spiritually engaged. That's not only going to make this effort work, bearing fruit for the glory of God; engaging your heart will help you grow spiritually.* These next few weeks will change your life, and the lives of others around you.

This manual is intended to equip you and your group to get the most out of this outreach effort. We will be engaging with teaching, Scripture, and discussion intended to move our hearts closer to God, closer to each other, and closer to the people whose lives we seek to bless. Each week (except week 1, which starts with the first group session) will start out with an introductory section to orient you to get the most out of that week's devotionals. This teaching is followed by five devotionals that you will do on your own. These devotionals will help prepare your heart and mind for the small group discussion on the topic for the upcoming week.

Each small group gathering will include a time of teaching by video, group discussion, prayer, and action steps. Completion of the devotionals should not be the determining factor for your attendance at that week's small group, but the devotionals will make this experience more powerful and the small group time most impactful.

**Three areas of your life will converge** or intersect for a new opportunity to live a more fruitful life as a follower of Jesus:

- Your church family
- Your everyday neighbors
- Your marginalized neighbors

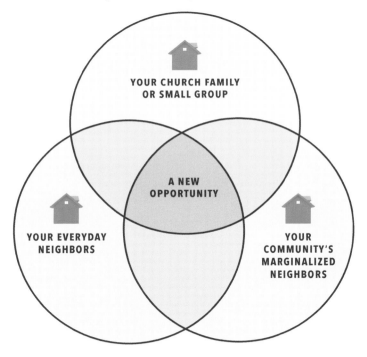

We call this "Convergence Evangelism" because it brings together at least three major spheres of your life. Where these three areas converge, we have a great opportunity to point others toward God. Our goal is to grow in our love for each of these circles, all in the context of growing in our love for God. We will live out some very specific ways of fulfilling the Great Commandments, to love God with all that we are, and to love our neighbors as we love ourselves (Mark 12:30-31). As we develop a heart for our church and our neighbors, we will find ourselves becoming more and more like Christ, which is God's goal for our lives.

## THE FIRST WHY: THE GREAT COMMISSION

If you knew you had only moments before you left this world and that you were entrusting the most important enterprise in human history to the people you were closest to in life, how significant would your final words be? You probably wouldn't waste those moments in small talk. You wouldn't say something that would distract your followers from their main mission. You would attempt to be clear and concise, straight to the point, right? Well, that's the situation Jesus faced before he ascended into heaven, after his death, burial, and resurrection. The best-known expression of those words is found in Matthew 28, verses that we know as the Great Commission.

> *Then Jesus came to them and said, "All authority in heaven and on earth has been given to me. Therefore go and make disciples of all nations, baptizing them in the name of the Father and of the Son and of the Holy Spirit, and teaching them to obey everything I have commanded you. And surely I am with you always, to the very end of the age." Matthew 28:18–20*

Jesus was entrusting the work of bringing the Good News of salvation for the whole world to his followers. We know from Luke's account in Acts 1:8 that the power behind the disciples' mission would be the Holy Spirit. Yet, Jesus was leaving the entire mission that he began in the hands of human beings. Now, in our own place and time, the mission has been entrusted to us. God has no other plan to bring about the redemption of lost, broken, and hurting humanity.

> *But you will receive power when the Holy Spirit comes on you; and you will be my witnesses in Jerusalem, and in all Judea and Samaria, and to the ends of the earth. Acts 1:8*

The one, primary command of Matthew 28:18 is this: "Make disciples." In the original Greek, this phrase is the only command. All the other verbs in the sentence have to do with how to make disciples: going, baptizing, and teaching. The inclusion of "baptizing" and "teaching" in the Great Commission means that making disciples is the work of the Church. So, even our personal witness as Christians must ultimately lead back to helping people become disciples in union with the church. If spreading the Good News, or evangelism, is the start of a process of discipleship that necessarily involves the local church,

**So, even our personal witness as Christians must ultimately lead back to helping people become disciples in union with the church.**

why not involve your local church from the beginning? Why not treat your witness as the team effort that making disciples entails? By working together with your church to invite your everyday neighbors to serve with you, you are moving those neighbors one step closer to glorifying God as disciples within God's family.

I've heard some people say that you're not really doing evangelism unless you personally lead people to pray to receive Jesus. Contrary to what some of us might feel, spreading the Good News is not a one-and-done proposition. Most people who receive Christ will do so only after multiple encounters with Christians and the message of the Good News. Convergence Evangelism doesn't purport to be the entire evangelism and discipleship package, but it is a powerful step toward enabling our neighbors to glorify God, in keeping with Matthew 5:16.

We also want to recognize that, for lots of different reasons, many believers are very uncomfortable with evangelism. Convergence Evangelism is evangelism for people without the gift of evangelism. Not only are we helping people take steps toward becoming followers of Christ, but we are also helping followers of Christ take steps toward becoming more comfortable with offering a witness. In our engagements with our neighbors while doing works of service, questions about our faith and hope will arise. We will more likely learn in this loving context that it's okay to give a gentle answer as to the reason for our hope.

*But in your hearts revere Christ as Lord. Always be prepared to give an answer to everyone who asks you to give the reason for the hope that you have. But do this with gentleness and respect, keeping a clear conscience, so that those who speak maliciously against your good behavior in Christ may be ashamed of their slander. 1 Peter 3:15-16*

In Luke's version of the Great Commission (Acts 1:8), Jesus sets forth the idea of different circles of responsibility where his followers would be his witnesses: Jerusalem, Judea and Samaria, and the ends of the earth. These circles suggest that you, too, have different circles of responsibility, different mission fields. The two we are focused on in Convergence Evangelism are your everyday neighbors and your neighbors who may live fairly close by, but who are marginal to your life, and maybe are more marginalized in our society.

## YOUR EVERYDAY NEIGHBORS

These are the people who constitute your everyday world: your friends, family, classmates, coworkers, and people in your neighborhood. They constitute a sphere of influence that you have that is unique to you. No one else on earth has the exact same web of relationships and connections. God has put you there for a reason. This is your world, and you are called to reach your world for Jesus.

Sometimes when we think of the Great Commission, we think of sending missionaries to distant parts of the globe. That's certainly important work, but supporting missionaries is not the only way to live out the Great Commission. When we think about reaching the entire world with the Good News of Jesus, that seems like such a huge task that we can easily absolve ourselves of any personal responsibility for it. Through this study and our outreach together, we're going to take responsibility for a little piece of our world. All of our efforts combined will make up a much larger share of completing our commission.

*Through this study and our outreach together, we're going to take responsibility for a little piece of our world.*

Most efforts to witness through our good deeds emphasize the witness we are making to those we are serving. There is absolutely nothing wrong with that. We celebrate the fact that churches are increasingly mobilizing their members to serve. Our good deeds speak the message of God's love and compassion to those we are serving. Good deeds should be backed up at some point by a verbal witness, but they can be vital in preparing the people we serve to receive the message that brings salvation. The people we serve, however, are not the only ones who receive the witness of our good deeds.

As we have seen, Jesus said in Matthew 5:16 that people who simply see, not necessarily receive, our good deeds will glorify the Father. That means that people who are not the recipients of our efforts can see what we do and be influenced toward God by our good deeds. The big question is, how are the people in your everyday world going to see your good works? Are they going to read about it in the news? Possibly, but not likely. Are you just going to tell them about your church's Saturday outreach on the Monday after? That might be good, but doesn't really let them see your good works. I can't think of a better way than to invite our unchurched neighbors to serve alongside us as we serve with our fellow Christ followers.

The big question is, how are the people in your everyday world going to see your good works?

We should know about our everyday neighbors who do not yet know Christ, that God has put something of his image in each one of them. Romans 2:15 says that "the requirements of the law are written on their hearts." That means that they have a capacity and desire to do good (and because they are a part of fallen humanity, they also have a capacity to do wrong, which is why they need the Good News). Those neighbors will not be made right with God simply by serving with you and your church family, but they will gain a sense that God has a higher purpose for their lives. Many of our everyday neighbors have their material needs met, but have fulfillment needs that only God can meet. *Serving alongside you will tap into their innate desire for a significant life.*

Also, many of your everyday neighbors view the church as irrelevant, and they think Christians are just judgmental. Your neighbors may also have some bad memories associated with their church experience. Some have given up on church. Many of them are more ready to serve with you than to worship with you. As a result of seeing you and your church in action, they will see a side of the church that is missing from many stereotypical views.

**Convergence Evangelism brings these dynamics into play with your everyday neighbors:**

1. They see your good works and move toward glorifying God (Matthew 5:16).

2. They become awakened to a higher purpose God has for them.

3. They have an opportunity to connect with loving Christians in a nonjudgmental, non-threatening environment.

4. They have an opportunity to witness in person the unity of the church and our love for one another within the family of God (see John 17:23).

Society recognizes that certain segments of our population are marginalized. That is, they live on the margins of society for a number of reasons, such as income or educational levels. Chances are, they are at the margins of our lives, too. While we are called to impact our everyday neighbors, we can't neglect our call to the margins.

Caring for the poor is a high scriptural priority. Unfortunately, for many decades much of the evangelical church world distanced itself from helping the poor. The reasoning was that many churches were not sharing the Good News of Jesus, perhaps not even believing in the need to do so, but they were caring for the poor through a "social gospel." What an unfortunate split in God's call for us to do both, share the message of Jesus and do the works of caring for people in need. Thankfully, in recent decades churches have renewed their commitments to both aspects of our witness.

We want to establish right from the beginning, however, that we are not asking you to serve marginalized people just because you're supposed to or just as a means of showing your everyday neighbors our good deeds. We must be operating out of love. Not only are we committed to the Great Commission, we are committed to the Great Commandments (Matthew 22:37-38), which include loving our neighbor as ourselves. Through our study, we are asking God to give us a heart for people who perhaps are too easily ignored. In the nice suburbs where the church I serve is located, we could easily avoid the needs of the impoverished community just a few minutes away. We have our separate school systems, and our major transit routes easily bypass that community. God hasn't bypassed the people there, and he wants us to show them that.

> *Jesus replied: "'Love the Lord your God with all your heart and with all your soul and with all your mind.' This is the first and greatest commandment. And the second is like it: 'Love your neighbor as yourself.'" Matthew 22:37-29*

John Maxwell has popularized the quote, "People don't care how much you know until they know how much you care."[1] This means if we want to share what we know about Jesus with our marginalized neighbors, we have to show how much we care first. Our day of service is about showing how much we care.

## YOUR CHURCH FAMILY

Some of the neighbors we want to learn to love more are the people of our own churches. When we work together in a project like this, moving from theory

---

[1] Maxwell, J. C. (2007). *The 21 Irrefutable Laws of Leadership: Follow Them and People Will Follow You*. New York, NY: HarperCollins Leadership.

into action, we have meaningful experiences that bring us closer together. Instead of risking conflict over minor points of teaching, or over relatively unimportant church decisions like the color of the carpet, we unite for what are some of the most important purposes of the church. We are bound together to fulfill our specific part of the Great Commission, and we learn to apply the Great Commandments, loving God and loving our neighbor.

We have noted the power of your neighbors' seeing your good deeds, moving them closer toward glorifying your Father in heaven. Another powerful set of dynamics comes into play when they see you with your church family. Jesus says in John 13:35 that people will know we are his disciples by our love for one another. That's important. However, in terms of moving your neighbors closer to God, there's an even more important aspect of your love for your church family: Jesus says in John 17:23 that by our unity, people will know that the Father has sent his Son. What a powerful witness, especially if our neighbors see a church of different ethnicities and walks of life working together in harmony. Our fractured society desperately needs the witness of Convergence Evangelism. Where else will our neighbors who are not yet ready to worship with us see this display of love and unity among God's family? Let's expect God to change lives through this effort, including our own.

> Jesus says in John 17:23 that by our unity people will know that the Father has sent his Son.

## VIDEO NOTES

## QUESTIONS FOR DISCUSSION

1. What about this study excited you? Why?
2. What about this study makes you nervous? Why?
3. Have you ever had a spiritual conversation with someone or invited them to church? How did it go?
4. Have you ever been a part of a service project before? Jesus says in Matthew 5:16 that people will see our good deeds and glorify our Father in heaven. Did your service project experience help that to happen? What could make our service projects more effective as a witness to our everyday neighbors?

## ACTION STEPS

1.  Write the name of someone to begin praying about inviting him/her to serve with you. This person should not yet be a follower of Jesus.

    _____

2.  Start to consider where you will serve. What service project will your group do? What is the date and time for your project? (See appendix for tips on conducting a service project.)
3.  Commit to complete the 5 devotionals on the next pages before we gather for Week 2 of small group.

## PRAY TOGETHER

**Pray this prayer together as a group:**

Heavenly Father,
We thank you for an opportunity to shine Your light to all of our neighbors. We thank you for the hope we have in Jesus, and we want that eternal hope for our neighbors. Open our hearts to the work you want to do in us and through us during these 6 weeks. Open the hearts of those we will invite to serve alongside us and those we will serve to experience your love. Please help us to be bold as we invite people.
Amen.

# DEVOTIONALS

## How to use these devotionals:

Begin by reading the introduction for the week. Each week will focus on one of your circles of influence or a Convergence Evangelism principle. This week, we will focus on God's call on our lives as followers of Jesus.

### TIME
Set aside 30 minutes during 5 days each week leading up to that week's small group session.

### LOCATION
Find a place where you can be alone and away from distraction. Take your Bible, this book, and a pen.

### ENGAGE IN REFLECTION
As you read through the devotional, there might be questions. Take time to think about your reflections on these questions. Jot them down in the notes section after each day if you'd like. Don't just breeze past them; push yourself to reflect.

### MEDITATE ON SCRIPTURE
Scripture readings will occur in different places each day. Take time to meditate on the Word of God. Maybe read the passage two or three times before you move on in the devotional.

### PRAY
Ask God what He is saying to you through the day's devotional and how He would like you to respond.

# YOU ARE SAVED TO SERVE

## GROUP SESSION 2

This week you will grow in your understanding that serving through good deeds is your destiny, and it's in your nature as a Christ-follower.

### INTRODUCTION TO THIS WEEK'S DEVOTIONALS

One of the primary questions, as we prepare for our day of service, is: Where will you serve? The goal for our devotionals this week is to help you understand that it is your destiny, and it is in your nature as a follower of Jesus to serve through good deeds.

If we are asking you to do good deeds, it's good to know that this is something you were saved to do. It's not just about a one-day service project.

This week we will look into Ephesians 2:10:

> *For we are God's handiwork, created in Christ Jesus to do good works, which God prepared in advance for us to do.*

This verse is so encouraging in what it says about who we are: "God's handiwork." I've heard whole sermons just on this amazing truth, sometimes using translations that even refer to us as "God's masterpiece."

A full understanding of Ephesians 2:10 requires us to move on to something else about us: we are saved to serve. Jesus doesn't save your soul just to take you to heaven. We are created in Christ to do good deeds while we are on this earth. This is your destiny. You are destined to make a difference in this world. Christians have varying views on the topic of predestination, but we can all agree that God has an amazing plan for your life that includes the good works you will be doing in connection with Convergence Evangelism. You are stepping into something that God has prepared in advance for you to do.

Don't downplay or underestimate what God can do through your direct acts of service for indi-

**We will be demonstrating great love to the people we serve. We will also be helping our everyday neighbors who serve with us.**

viduals and organizations that serve our marginalized neighbors. It's true that direct help doesn't always address the systemic needs of our cities and neighborhoods, but we are expecting great things from God through our efforts. Mother Teresa rightly states, "Not all of us can do great things, but we can do small things with great love." We will be demonstrating great love to the people we serve. We will also be helping our everyday neighbors who serve with us.

Biju Thampy, an Indian pastor and founder of Vision Rescue, shares about the time he was being awakened by the Lord to the needs of the community. Biju was hesitant to tackle the poverty he was witnessing because he knew it required systemic change. But he felt that the Lord was asking him, "What would you do if it was your own child who was hungry?" Biju responded, "I would give him something to eat." So, even though he knew that feeding a few children wouldn't change the system and really address the needs of the whole person, he realized that God was telling him to start with what he had and with what he could do. Now, in addition to direct aid to the poor, the emphasis of Biju's organization is primarily on education and helping those children to really have a chance in life, but it all started with just handing out food to hungry street children. It all started with simply doing good deeds.

When we embrace God's call to serve a community in need, we will be helping in small ways that may ultimately have a huge impact. We will also be living out a major purpose of our salvation in Jesus Christ.

## DAY 1 | YOU ARE CREATED TO DO GOOD WORKS.

> *For we are God's handiwork, created in Christ Jesus to do good works, which God prepared in advance for us to do. Ephesians 2:10*

You are made for this! That is, you are God's handiwork. God is working in you to shape you increasingly to be like Jesus. If you are a follower of Jesus, God is working in you in such a way as to make doing his will your personal ambition (see Philippians 2:13). You have no reason to be intimidated in this endeavor, even if you are stepping out of your comfort zone. You and the people with whom you are learning and serving are created in Christ Jesus for this moment.

The challenge is not too great, nor is the task too small to be meaningful. This story in Acts 9 has a great lesson for us on the great potential for small tasks:

> *In Joppa there was a disciple named Tabitha (in Greek her name is Dorcas); she was always doing good and helping the poor. About that time she became sick and died, and her body was washed and placed in an upstairs room. Lydda was near Joppa; so when the disciples heard that Peter was in Lydda, they sent two men to him and urged*

*him, "Please come at once!" Peter went with them, and when he arrived he was taken upstairs to the room. All the widows stood around him, crying and showing him the robes and other clothing that Dorcas had made while she was still with them. Peter sent them all out of the room; then he got down on his knees and prayed. Turning toward the dead woman, he said, "Tabitha, get up." She opened her eyes, and seeing Peter she sat up. He took her by the hand and helped her to her feet. Then he called for the believers, especially the widows, and presented her to them alive. This became known all over Joppa, and many people believed in the Lord. Acts 9:36–42*

Dorcas made clothing. She must have made a lot of clothing! Still, providing clothing is a relatively small thing compared with the major miracles of Jesus and the apostles. It might not be as spiritual as other works. It might be a small thing in the view of people who only consider a systemic change to be worthwhile. But providing clothing was probably what Dorcas was made for. She was displaying God's handiwork, not just her own. The results were that Dorcas was raised from the dead, many people believed in Jesus, and Peter's ministry became established in Joppa. We can't minimize the potential impact of the small things we do.

1. What does it mean when it says we are God's handiwork or workmanship?

2. What are some of the good works God created us to do? Does it matter if the good works are small? Why or why not?

3. The verse says God has prepared good works in advance for us to do. What does that say about your destiny? Is it easier to do a good work that you know God has already prepared for you to do? Why or why not?

## DAY 2 | FAITH WITHOUT WORKS IS DEAD.

The Apostle Paul, who is introduced to us in the Book of Acts and who went on to write much of the New Testament, had tried to make himself right with God by good works. His emphasis was not so much on good deeds as on religious works, rituals, and so forth—even to the point of persecuting Christians.

Paul came up empty in his search for God until Jesus revealed himself to Paul, and Paul made a discovery: Jesus had made Paul right with God through his death on the cross, and all Paul had to do was receive salvation by faith.

*For it is by grace you have been saved, through faith—and this is not from yourselves, it is the gift of God— not by works, so that no one can boast. Ephesians 2:8-9*

Yet, as we have seen already and as Paul says in the very next verse, we are created in Christ to do good works.

So, while we acknowledge salvation is by faith and not by our works, it's vital that we understand that faith and works are not opposed to each other. One should lead to the other; that is, faith should lead to good works. As a person of faith, you demonstrate your faith through your works. If we don't have the kind of faith that leads to doing good deeds of love for others, James tells us our faith is dead:

*What good is it, my brothers and sisters, if someone claims to have faith but has no deeds? Can such faith save them? Suppose a brother or a sister is without clothes and daily food. If one of you says to them, "Go in peace; keep warm and well fed," but does nothing about their physical needs, what good is it? In the same way, faith by itself, if it is not accompanied by action, is dead. James 2:14–17*

## IMPORTANT IMPLICATIONS FOR CONVERGENCE EVANGELISM:

1. Our good deeds are an expression of our faith in Jesus. If we trust Jesus for our salvation, we will show it in good deeds.

2. Our good deeds don't save us.

3. The good deeds of the people who are serving alongside us are not sufficient to bring them salvation. We are, however, moving them closer to salvation by showing our good deeds as followers of Jesus.

4. Remember Matthew 5:16: People will see our good deeds and glorify our Father in heaven.

If you have not yet received God's free gift of salvation—being made right with God—by putting your faith in Jesus' sacrifice on the cross, right now would be a great time to do so. Today is your day! I invite you to make this prayer your own:

> God, I thank you for sending your Son. I believe Jesus died, that he was raised from the dead, and that he is Lord. Forgive me of my sins, be the Lord of my life, and help me live for you. Thank you for saving me. Amen.

If you are new to faith in Jesus or you're making a fresh commitment to follow Jesus, be sure to ask your group leader, or another leader in a Bible-believing church, about appropriate next steps.

> *If you declare with your mouth, "Jesus is Lord," and believe in your heart that God raised him from the dead, you will be saved. For it is with your heart that you believe and are justified, and it is with your mouth that you profess your faith and are saved. Romans 10:9-10*

## FOR REFLECTION:

What are some evidences of your faith in God? Are good deeds among them?

## DAY 3 | BE WHO JESUS SAYS YOU ARE.

Convergence Evangelism hinges on doing the good works that God has prepared in advance for us to do (Ephesians 2:10). We are putting our faith into action. Something that's perhaps even more important than what we do, however, is who we are. Several passages put our "being" before our "doing." We are to be worshipers, since the Father is seeking worshipers, not seeking worship (John 4:23). We are empowered to be witnesses, not just to witness (Acts 1:8). We worship because we are worshipers. We witness because God has made us his witnesses. We shine through our good deeds because God has made us the light of the world! Look what Jesus says about you:

> *You are the salt of the earth. But if the salt loses its saltiness, how can it be made salty again? It is no longer good for anything, except to be thrown out and trampled underfoot. You are the light of the world. A town built on a hill cannot be hidden. Neither do people light a lamp and put it under a bowl. Instead they put it on its stand, and it gives light to everyone in the house. In the same way, let your light shine before others, that they may see your good deeds and glorify your Father in heaven. Matthew 5:13–16*

You are the salt of the earth. You are the light of the world. You are a city on a hill. This is your identity as a follower of Jesus. We might think that this identity only pertains to the first disciples and that we could never measure up to that standard. Jesus didn't say these words to the apostles as we usually think of them. He said this at the very beginning of his ministry. They hadn't done any ministry yet. The full cohort of disciples hadn't even been gathered yet. We also know that this sermon, the Sermon on the Mount, was heard by the crowds, and it applies to us today. So, you are the salt of the earth. You are the light of the world.

Our primary responsibility, according to these verses, is just to stay salty and to refuse to cover up our light. Part of staying salty is being genuinely good people, which is made possible because of the love of Jesus in our hearts. We aren't just doing good works in order to cover up our character flaws! So, stay salty.

Also, let your light be seen. We can't hide under a bowl. We have to get out there. Then simply shine. It's not that radical. It's not that hard to do. Just be. Together, as God's church, we are indeed a town on a hill that cannot be hidden. Let's shine.

---

**FOR REFLECTION:**

What does it mean to put the primary emphasis on who you are, not just what you do? How might this emphasis make it easier for you to do good deeds for others?

---

## DAY 4 | YOUR PATHWAY TO GREATNESS.

God has created you to be great. You may not attain greatness as the world defines greatness, but you were created for a great God, and through Christ, that great God lives in you. That means you have greatness within you!

Our good deeds done in service to others are God's way of bringing his greatness out of you. When we try to attain greatness for ourselves by striving and straining in the self-centered way that dominates our society, we become unhealthy. We too often experience the unhealthy effects of our striving in our bodies, our emotions, and our spirits. We must go after greatness God's way.

Two of Jesus' main disciples, James and John, requested that Jesus give them positions of greatness in Jesus' coming kingdom. James and John were misguided in both their understanding of Jesus' kingdom and how to attain greatness in it. Here's what's crazy about this story: Jesus didn't rebuke James and John for their desire for greatness. Instead, Jesus told them the one way to become great:

> Whoever wants to become great among you must be your servant. Mark 10:43b

Jesus challenged their misunderstanding, but he still pointed his disciples toward greatness. Service is the path to greatness. James and John wanted a shortcut, but there are no shortcuts. Convergence Evangelism that engages you in serving others can be a major force for your advancement to greatness, for your emotional and spiritual health, and for making a significant difference in your world.

Because God has placed an inner desire for

greatness within you as a follower of Jesus, you have an inner drive to do acts of service. Paul says this about the kind of people we are:

> *[Jesus] gave himself for us to redeem us from all wickedness and to purify for himself a people that are his very own, eager to do what is good.*
> Titus 2:14

"Eager to do what is good" literally means "zealous for good works" (Titus 2:14 ESV). Martin Luther King Jr. said this about greatness, "Everybody can be great because anybody can serve. You don't have to have a college degree to serve. You don't have to make your subject and verb agree to serve. You only need a heart full of grace. A soul generated by love."

Jesus has placed his zeal for good works in you. He has filled your heart with his grace and love. It's up to you to let it out.

## FOR REFLECTION:

In what ways does God want you to be great? How does the greatness God has for you differ from the usual concept of greatness? Are you eager to do good works? Do you have room to grow in eagerness?

You, as followers of Jesus, are hereby officially authorized to annoy each other. Well, maybe not annoy, but certainly to provoke. I say that because of this verse:

*And let us consider how we may spur one another on toward love and good deeds. Hebrews 10:24*

The word translated "spur" is usually used with a negative connotation. It generally has to do with irritating and provoking. So why would the writer use such a word here, especially with regard to how we are to treat one another within the family of God? It's because love and good deeds are not optional. While we are making it as easy and natural as possible through Convergence Evangelism, the reality is that good deeds are easy to neglect. We get busy with our lives and can forget about the people who need our good deeds and who need the witness for Christ that our good deeds bring. So the Bible frees us up to spur or urge one another toward what we really want to do anyway.

Another thing that this verse lets us know is that our good deeds are not just an individual project. Yes, we as individuals would do well to be doing good deeds whenever and wherever we can. You, as an individual, are definitely made for good works. We should not limit ourselves to individualized action, though. We are in this together.

Notice this about Hebrews 10:24: We are actually supposed to give some thought and consideration as to how we can spur one another on. This is what we are doing right now through this Convergence Evangelism endeavor. Your participation in your daily reading and in your small group is a chance to put this verse into practice. Don't be too irritating, but don't let yourself or others off the hook too easily!

---

**FOR REFLECTION:**

Think about what you can do to provoke others to love and good works. How can you put this into practice in your church or small group?

# ⌂ WEEK 2 | SMALL GROUP

## VIDEO NOTES

## QUESTIONS FOR DISCUSSION

1. When you hear the phrase "good deeds," what deeds do you associate with it and why? What is the connection between doing good deeds and loving our neighbors?
2. What new insights did you gain about being saved to serve? What questions do you have from your devotionals this week? What points of reflection really challenged or helped you?
3. In what ways do you find yourself serving yourself on a daily basis?
4. In what ways do you find yourself serving God on a daily basis?

5. Share about a time you did a good deed for someone you didn't know. How did it make you feel?
6. What holds you back from doing good deeds?

## ACTION STEPS

1. Choose your service project.
2. Write the name of someone to begin praying about inviting him/her to serve with you. This person should not yet be a follower of Jesus. Write this name on a post-it note and share it with a partner – the who and why you chose this person.
3. Commit to complete the 5 devotionals on the next pages before we gather for Week 3 of small group.

## PRAY TOGETHER

On a post-it-note or index card, jot the name of someone you'd like to invite to serve alongside you. Gather in groups of three to pray for the person on each of your cards.

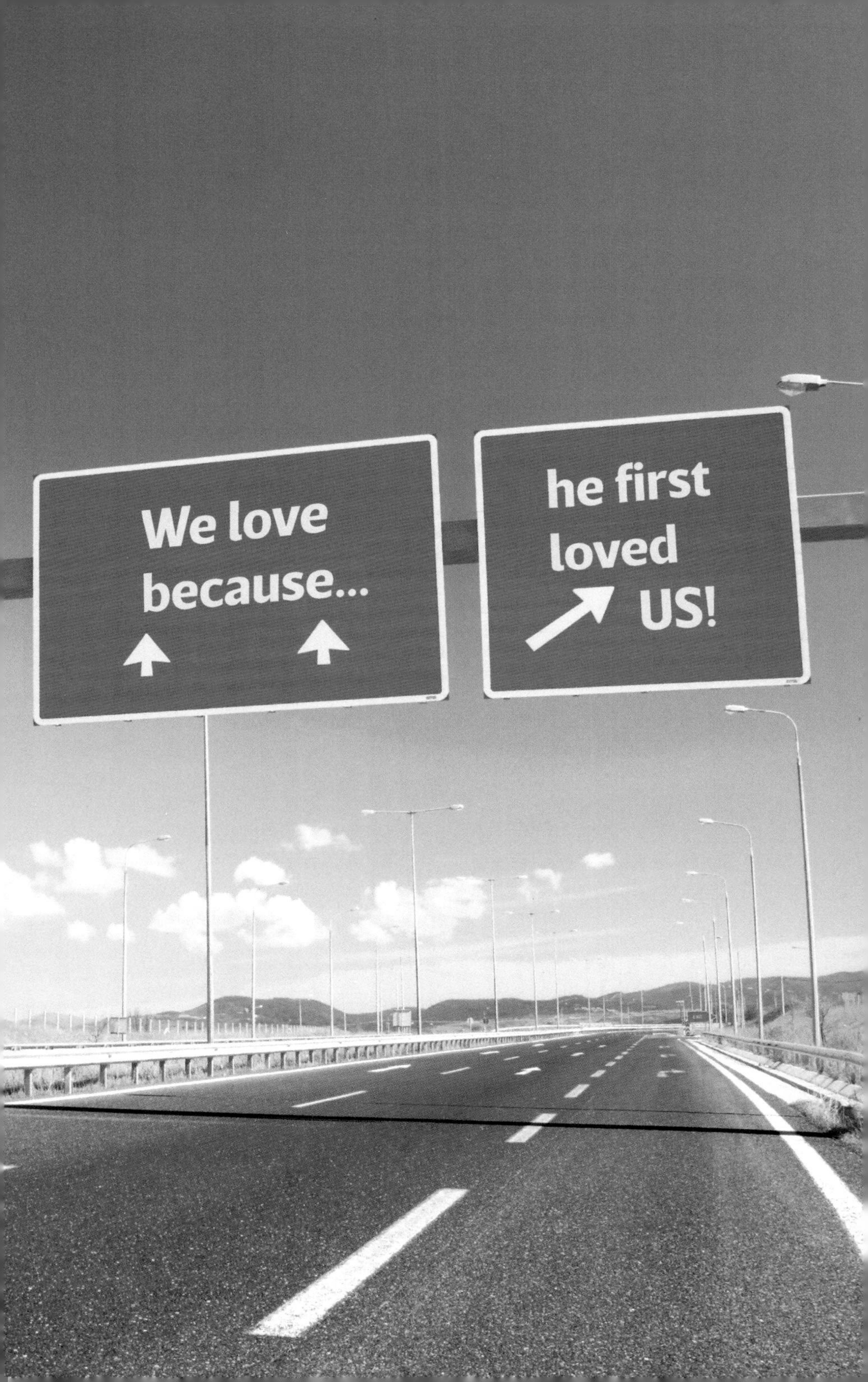
We love because...
he first loved US!

# 3

# A HEART FOR YOUR EVERYDAY NEIGHBORS

## GROUP SESSION 3

This week you will grow in love for and in understanding the needs of your everyday neighbors.

### INTRODUCTION TO THIS WEEK'S DEVOTIONALS

> *And let us consider how we may spur one another on toward love and good deeds. Hebrews 10:24*

God has given you a very unique assignment. No one else has exactly the same set of relationships that you do. You have connections with people that your pastor or other spiritual leaders do not have. Your connections with your friends, family members, coworkers, fellow students, and others whose lives intersect with yours form a sphere of influence for which God gives you a degree of responsibility. These are your everyday neighbors. For many of these people, you are their best hope for getting to know God. You might be the only follower of Jesus they know.

A lot of us want to share our faith but are very uncomfortable doing so. We can be especially uncomfortable sharing our faith with the people we personally care about the most. Maybe we have shared our faith with family and coworkers many times, and we feel we aren't being heard anymore. Maybe we have invited them to church already, but they don't seem interested. Convergence Evangelism is designed with these neighbors of yours in mind.

> It's part of their God-given destiny, and we should not be surprised that people are attracted to their God-given destinies, even before they know God.

**Many of your everyday neighbors are not ready to worship with you, but they are ready to serve with you.** God has put within them a desire to do something significant. Your invitation to serve appeals to that desire. We are actually inviting unbelievers to begin moving toward the good works that God has prepared in advance for them to do. It's part of their God-given destiny, and we should not be surprised that people are attracted to their God-given destinies, even before they know God. We are God's handiwork, and he doesn't start his work just when we get saved.

Many of your everyday neighbors aren't responsive to your words about God and your faith.

Jesus tells us that they will see your good works and glorify your Father in heaven (Matthew 5:16). By serving with you, they will receive a witness of the light of Jesus that shines through you.

Many of your everyday neighbors only know what the church stands against. By serving with you, they will see the love of God in action. Jesus says that people will know the Father has sent the Son when they see our unity (John 17:23). How will your everyday neighbors see the unity of followers of Jesus? They might not be ready to see it in a worship service, but if your service is part of a church or group project, they will see it when they serve with you.

Ask God to help you grow in your love for and understanding of the people in your everyday life. God wants to bless them through you. Convergence Evangelism is one way God can do that.

## DAY 1 | YOUR NEIGHBOR HAS A HIGHER CALLING.

Do you ever have a problem finding a gift for that person in your life who seems to have everything? My parents, for example, are not wealthy by any means, but they are also at a stage in life where they just don't need much of what I might want to give them for Christmas. We might have the same challenge with identifying the needs of people in our everyday world.

Needs-meeting ministries are so important for the church. We feed the hungry, care for orphans and widows, provide comfort in grief, and serve where the needs are often quite obvious. But what do we provide for our everyday neighbors who don't have such obvious needs? They aren't immune to tragedy, but how do we serve in between troubled times? The more affluent our everyday neighbors are, the more likely that they have no pressing needs for our typical good works.

Still, everyone has needs of some kind. Even our everyday neighbors who seem as though life is going their way have needs. The needs that surveys of suburban America often reveal are of a more emotional or spiritual-type: a need for significance, a need for fulfillment.

We are expecting and praying for life change for the neighbors we invite to serve with us. The life change we offer people in Jesus is not only about stopping certain behavior, however. Sometimes the life change is to start doing something more significant than what they have been doing. Jesus' call to Peter is a great example:

> *Passing alongside the Sea of Galilee, he saw Simon and Andrew the brother of Simon casting a net into the sea, for they were fishermen. And Jesus said to them, "Follow me, and I will make you become fishers of men." And immediately they left their nets and followed him. And going on a little farther, he saw James the son of Zebedee and John his brother, who were in their boat mending the nets. And immediately he called them, and they left their father Zebedee in the boat with the hired servants and followed him. Mark 1:16–20 (ESV)*

Jesus' call was so appealing that the response was immediate. Notice this about the call: Peter's call was to a higher level of significance.

Many of your everyday neighbors know the church only for what we oppose. Are we against certain things? Yes. We are against injustice. We are against behaviors that devalue life and devalue the individual. We are against behaviors that destroy community, that break down families, that harm our children, that harm ourselves. But, if we are to reach our neighbors with the Good News of Jesus, we can't exclusively focus on what we are against.

Also, too many people see turning to God as having to give up something. Yes, it is that, but it's so much more. God does not have you or your neighbor give up something without replacing it with something much more, usually infinitely more, fulfilling and satisfying. So our focus is not on what we're against, or what we ought to give up, or what we have given up. Our focus is on what God has given us, on what he is calling our neighbors and us to do. Our focus is the higher calling of God. God is not interested in just stopping our bad behavior; God is calling us to something else that is so much better.

Peter accepted the high calling. He left everything to follow Jesus. **When you invite your seemingly need-free neighbors to serve alongside you, our expectation is that they will begin to hear Jesus' call to something more satisfying and significant.**

Your everyday neighbors need that. Let's meet them at their point of need.

### DAY 2 | YOUR NEIGHBOR WAS CREATED TO DO GOOD.

Ecclesiastes 3:11 says that God "has planted eternity in the human heart" (NLT). The passage says this in the context of our work here on earth, including doing good:

> *I know that there is nothing better for people than to be happy and to do good while they live.*
> *Ecclesiastes 3:11*

Doing good will not give us, or our everyday neighbors, a full picture of who God is and what he has done for us. Only in Jesus do we begin to grasp the enormity of God's work on behalf of humanity. Yet, when we do good, we tap into the yearning for eternity that God has planted in every human heart. Our everyday neighbors aren't just called to a more significant life here on earth; they are called to eternity.

Part of the reason that doing good is connected to having eternity in our hearts is that God is good, God does good, and we are made in God's image. While sin has distorted the image of God in humanity, there's a sufficient connection to eternity within each person to give us a yearning for it. **When we invite our everyday neighbors to serve with us, we give them an opportunity to act on something God has put within them.** This is especially true considering they will see our love for God, our love for each other, and our love for our neighbors.

By nature, people who do not yet follow Jesus sometimes do good and give evidence that God has written his law on their hearts (Romans 2:14-15). Paul makes clear in Romans that their salvation is found only through faith in Christ, not in their good works, but he certainly does affirm the good they do as evidence of God's handiwork. Because of what God has already put within your everyday neighbors, they are more inclined to serve alongside you than we perhaps realize. That's why some of our neighbors are more ready to serve with you than to worship with you.

Let's also keep in mind that as we invite our neighbors to serve alongside us, we aren't just trying to make them feel good about themselves. We are witnesses through our own good works, and through the good works, our neighbors will see many of our fellow Christians doing. The end result goes back to Matthew 5:16: They will see our good works and glorify our Father in heaven.

FOR REFLECTION:

Think about the person you are inviting to serve with you. Ask God to help you see them the way God sees them. What does it mean for that person to be made in the image of God?

## DAY 3 | YOUR EVERYDAY NEIGHBOR HAS SPIRITUAL NEEDS.

Not only do our everyday neighbors have needs for fulfillment or a capacity to do good. They also have spiritual needs that only Jesus can meet. It's sometimes too easy to think only people with material needs have spiritual needs.

If we are honest, sometimes we're more comfortable reaching out to marginalized people because we feel superior. We are intimidated by people we consider to be at or above our own social standing. If we are to address the spiritual needs of our everyday neighbors, we should quit rating ourselves or others on any kind of value scale based on social standing. There is no difference in Christ. That should keep us from feeling inferior to some, superior to others. It will also keep us from being intimidated by people of our own standing in society, freeing us to love them and be witnesses to them.

Some church people may have questions about the propriety of inviting people who do not yet follow Jesus to serve with us. After all, Paul warns in 2 Corinthians 6:14 against being unequally yoked. We are not, however, inviting people to be yoked with us. **We are instead being very intentional about helping our near neighbors to hear the call of Jesus to take on his yoke.**

Jesus says this:

> "Come to me, all you who are weary and burdened, and I will give you rest. Take my yoke upon you and learn from me, for I am gentle and humble in heart, and you will find rest for your souls. Matthew 11:28-29

We are not focusing on our partnership with our everyday neighbors in serving, as important as that is. It's not about us. We are focusing on letting Jesus work through us to call people who are weary and burdened to come to him. In serving our marginalized neighbors, we are the hands and feet of Jesus. **Also, we are going to be the mouthpiece for Jesus,**

**who calls the world, including our everyday neighbors, to take on his yoke.**

I suspect that behind the "success" of lots of our everyday neighbors, especially those of greater affluence, you will find a good bit of weariness along with emotional and spiritual burdens.

Jesus' yoke is for the weary and burdened—for people who have been trying to plow through life on their own. Perhaps your neighbors are trying to live good lives apart from God but feel weary and burdened. Jesus offers them rest, but he offers it with a yoke. A yoke is an instrument of labor and signifies laboring with Jesus. **Jesus has something for your neighbors to do in partnership with himself! Jesus is setting the course and the pace.** We are yoked with Jesus. We are encouraging our neighbors to take on Jesus' yoke, too.

## FOR REFLECTION:

Pray for the spiritual needs of the person you are inviting to serve with you. What kinds of stresses and burdens is that person carrying? Pray that they will be able to trade these yokes for the yoke and rest Jesus has for them and that they would truly learn from Jesus. Pray that they will see that Jesus is gentle and humble in heart.

What do people in your community think about the church and about Christians? Even in parts of the country where church-going is more common, lots of people know very little about followers of Jesus. People may have very little exposure to Christianity, and when they do, the exposure is negative. Maybe they only know the stereotypes of harsh, judgmental attitudes, or they associate Christianity with a particular political position. So many people only know what the newspapers say about Christians, and too often, that's a story about the moral failure of a church leader. You might be the only real exposure people have to Christianity.

Your life is a light to your neighbors. They need your light, and they need to see good deeds that will cause them to glorify your Father. In 1 Peter 2:12, Peter echoes the words of Jesus that we read in Matthew 5:16.

> *Live such good lives among the pagans that, though they accuse you of doing wrong, they may see your good deeds and glorify God on the day he visits us.*

Our good deeds will speak more loudly than our political arguments or our judgmental attitudes. Peter also suggests that, along with our good deeds, we witness by explaining the reason for our hope when people ask about it:

> *But in your hearts revere Christ as Lord. Always be prepared to give an answer to everyone who asks you to give the reason for the hope that you have. But do this with gentleness and respect. 1 Peter 3:16*

Are the people of our community seeing our hope?

I was participating in a prayer event on the steps outside the county courthouse, and my assignment was to pray for justice. My goal was to pray a prayer that would not be overtly political and could be agreed to by a very diverse group of Christian clergy. After the prayer, a passerby who happened to hear me said, "I'm for justice, but probably not the kind of justice you're for." My words about justice might have connected with God, but they did not connect with that person. She really didn't have a clue as to what I stood for; all she had to go on were my words.

Let's be honest: our words can too easily be controversial and divisive in today's social climate. People make assumptions about our words that may or may not be accurate. Our words don't always connect the way we want them to. Since our church has ramped up our direct service to the needs of the city, however, our deeds have connected with people of all persuasions. Giving a homeless person a coat to keep warm in winter speaks in a way that my words don't.

If your church is multiethnic, or your day of service is being conducted by multiple churches across ethnic lines, your neighbors will see a witness of love and unity they rarely see anywhere else. The church I serve is very multiethnic, but unless our neighbors attend a worship service, they receive very little witness of the unity Christ brings across societal divides. Since some people are more ready to serve with us than to worship with us, a multiethnic outreach sends a powerful message of Christ's love (see John 17:23). That message goes out not only to the people we serve but to the people who serve alongside us.

Through your inviting your everyday neighbors to serve with you, they are going to see a side of our faith that perhaps they have never seen before. Your good deeds and your love for your church family will speak more loudly to them than judgmental attitudes or political arguments, whether of the right or of the left. We should be aware that at some point, words about the Good News of Jesus will have to be shared for our neighbors to come to salvation. You might not be the one to share those words, but your deeds will make way for those words to be received.

## FOR REFLECTION:

Pray that the person you're inviting to serve with you will see the church and our good deeds in a way that glorifies God. Pray that as they interact with followers of Christ, they will see the hope that we have. Pray also that our answers to their questions would be given with gentleness and respect.

Did you receive Christ the first time the Good News was presented to you? Probably not. People usually need multiple encounters with God, his family, his witnesses, and the Good News before they are ready to say yes to Jesus. Paul says this about his mission of spreading the Good News:

> *I planted the seed, Apollos watered it, but God has been making it grow. 1 Corinthians 3:6*

The Bible suggests a process for people to come into a full relationship with God when Paul writes of some planting, some watering, then God giving the increase. That agricultural image runs counter to any ideas that we just share our witness, and people immediately respond. Even the crowds that responded to Peter on the day of Pentecost had been exposed to the teaching of the Old Covenant. When Paul went into a city to spread the Good News, he would typically go to the synagogues and the places of prayer where people were somewhat prepared for the message already. Paul spent months in one place trying to persuade people. In Acts 18:4, we see that Paul reasoned in the synagogue week after week, trying to persuade Jews and Greeks. Paul did the same in Acts 19:8, for a period of three months. In Acts 26:28, Agrippa wondered if Paul could convert him in such a short time. All these examples indicate a process for people to receive Christ. When we invite our neighbors to serve with us, we are inviting our neighbors into a biblical process that will prepare them for what God wants to do in their lives.

Inviting someone to serve with you doesn't complete the work of evangelism and of making disciples. It does, however, expose our everyday neighbors to the dynamics that Scripture says will witness of God's love to them. Particularly important, inviting someone to serve with you exposes our neighbors to our good deeds and, when we serve with our church family, to our love for one another. Paul didn't do it all by himself; Apollos had a role, too. We will be more effective by working together.

We are most effective in our witness, whether through words or deeds, when we trust God with the process. Sure, we have to do our part, but God is the one who makes the seed grow. Keep in mind that God is probably already working in the life of the person you are inviting to serve with you, meaning you may not be the first person in their process of coming to know Christ. That also means the person you are inviting might be far more ready to serve with you than you know. Continue to grow in your expectation for God to work in you and through you, but don't put too much pressure on yourself. We can count on God to do what he has committed himself to do.

## FOR REFLECTION:

Reflect on the thought that you are part of a process for other people to become followers of Jesus. How does that make you feel concerning your role? How does it feel to know that God is the one who ultimately makes the process work?

## VIDEO NOTES

## QUESTIONS FOR DISCUSSION

1. When you think about your everyday neighbors, who comes to mind?
2. What are the greatest needs of your everyday neighbors? Do you think they tend to be material needs, relational needs, fulfillment needs, or something else?
3. Do your everyday neighbors seem to be interested in spiritual things? Why or why not?
4. In what ways have you tried to be a light or witness to your neighbors in the past?
5. God has placed within every human being a capacity to do good. How do you see your everyday

neighbors living that out? How can inviting them to serve with you help them move toward God's plans for their lives?

## ACTION STEPS

1. Make an invitation to serve to your neighbor you identified from Week 2. See the script in the Appendix for help on what to say.
2. Pray daily for a friend to be blessed and respond to the invitation.
3. Commit to complete the five devotionals on the next pages before we gather for Week 4 of small group.

## PRAY TOGETHER

Pray as a whole group for those who you are inviting to serve alongside you.

BE SOMEBODY
WHO MAKES
EVERYBODY
FEEL LIKE A
SOMEBODY

# 4

# A HEART FOR YOUR MARGINAL NEIGHBORS

## GROUP SESSION 4

This week you will grow in your genuine concern for people in need and on the margins of society.

### INTRODUCTION TO THIS WEEK'S DEVOTIONALS

We have looked at the fact that we are saved to serve. This week, let's look at the heart and attitudinal aspects of the call to serve people in need. **Instead of just looking at God's call on us to serve, let's look at God's heart for the people we are called to serve.**

Our service can't be a show for our marginalized neighbors. It can't just be a show for our everyday neighbors. Anyone can plop food on a plate at a feeding center without caring for or honoring the people being served. Convergence Evangelism is about serving our fellow human beings with love in a way that offers as much dignity as possible.

For Matthew 5:16 to work, our deeds must be truly good in the biblical sense of the word "good": lovely, praiseworthy, excellent, representing an inner character of goodness. We want our neighbors to sense the heart of Jesus in our ministry to and with them.

We should be attentive to the ways God can work through us to move people from the margins of society. We want to help in a way that advances people's lives. We want to move them from the margins into our churches if they do not have a church family of their own. Sometimes this step will be in partnership with other churches in the neighborhoods where they live.

> Our service can't be a show for our marginalized neighbors. It can't just be a show for our everyday neighbors.

A heartfelt desire to move people from the margins toward being fully empowered members of the community will sometimes result in the development of ministries and efforts that address systemic issues. These efforts go beyond the scope of Convergence Evangelism, but our hope is that the more we as the church are exposed to marginalized people and their issues, the more we will be motivated to get involved at deeper levels.

We also sincerely desire that some of our everyday neighbors will continue to extend resources toward the marginalized. This will bridge some of the divides that plague our nation and increase meaningful dialogue and interaction. Our world desperately needs to see what God will do when his people really care about people in need and are moved to do something about it. Isaiah 58 tells us that if we will pour ourselves out to feed, clothe, and shelter people in need, this will happen:

> *Then your light will break forth like the dawn, and your healing will quickly appear; then your righteousness will go before you, and the glory of the LORD will be your rear guard. Isaiah 58:8*

There is something supernatural happening here, and we can't underestimate the Spirit's power to make happen what the Bible says will happen. I believe that what Jesus said is true: people will see our good works and glorify our Father in heaven. The Holy Spirit will be working through us to draw people toward God.

We want all people involved in our outreach, that is, our fellow church volunteers, our everyday neighbors, and our marginalized neighbors, to be drawn closer to God. Let's do our best this week to allow God to expand our love for our marginalized neighbors.

The marginalized people we serve are not props for a show we put on to impress our everyday neighbors. If we treat them as such, we will have no real impact on either our marginalized neighbors or our everyday neighbors who are serving with us.

Our key verse for Convergence Evangelism is Matthew 5:16, in which **Jesus explicitly commands us to do good deeds that are to be seen by people**, leading them to glorify our Father in heaven. Just a few verses later, in the very same sermon, Jesus warns against doing good deeds as a show.

> *Watch out! Don't do your good deeds publicly, to be admired by others, for you will lose the reward from your Father in heaven. (Matthew 6:1 NLT).*

Which way is it? Do we do good deeds publicly or not? The issue here is the condition of our hearts and our goals for doing good deeds. We actually could have two people doing the exact same kind of good deed, but one deed leads to no reward at all, and the other leads to God being glorified. One person might be saying through their good deeds, "Admire me," while the other is saying, "Admire God! Glorify God!" With Convergence Evangelism, we are saying through our good deeds, "Look how much God loves you," not, "See how good we are."

We aren't even trying to say, "See how much we love you." Yes, we do love the people we are serving, and there's nothing wrong with people knowing that, but our primary goal is for people to know that God loves them. Through our serving, we are conduits for God's love to the hurting.

> *Dear friends, let us love one another, for love comes from God. Everyone who loves has been born of God and knows God. 1 John 4:7*

The love we share with our marginalized neighbors comes from God, too. In fact, God so closely relates to the poor that when we serve the poor, it's like lending to God himself! Being kind to the poor honors God.

> *Dear friends, let us love one another, for love comes from God. Everyone who loves has been born of God and knows God. 1 John 4:7*

> *Whoever oppresses the poor shows contempt for their Maker, but whoever is kind to the needy honors God. Proverbs 14:31*

Let's ask God to give us his heart and to help us grow in our love for the people God loves and cares for so much.

## DAY 2 | LOVING MEANS DOING.

God loves in ways that go beyond words. God loves
by doing. God loved by sending his Son:

> *For God so loved the world that he gave his one
> and only Son, that whoever believes in him shall
> not perish but have eternal life. John 3:16*

God loves by blessing, saving, rescuing. And so
should we.

We have looked at the relationship between
faith and works, described by James in James 2:14-
17, where James says, "faith by itself, if it is not accompanied by action, is dead." James is emphatic that

we must provide for people in need, not just speak a religious-sounding blessing over them.

In the verses before this passage, James is challenging the church not to show favoritism toward the rich. He points out in verse 5 the special place the poor have in God's plan of salvation. James then says this in verse 8:

> *If you really keep the royal law found in Scripture, "Love your neighbor as yourself," you are doing right. James 2:8*

When Jesus spoke of the "royal law," the religious people wanted to limit the implications of the law for themselves by narrowly defining who their neighbors were. Jesus' response to their self-serving limit on love was the Parable of the Good Samaritan (Luke 10:25-37). Showing mercy, actually doing something for a neighbor in need, is Jesus' prescribed way of fulfilling the second of the Great Commandments: love your neighbor as yourself.

Our doing good is not just proof of our faith; it is a demonstration of love. We are indeed more concerned that people know that God loves them, but we also want to fulfill God's command for us to love them, too.

> *Dear children, let us not love with words or speech but with actions and in truth. 1 John 3:18*

For God, his love for us goes far beyond words. Our love for others must be more than words, too.

**FOR REFLECTION:**

Pray about the marginalized people of our community or region. Pray for the churches and agencies that serve their needs. Pray that we could come alongside those churches and agencies in a way that demonstrates a love that goes beyond words.

## DAY 3 | WE MUST LOVE ACROSS THE BARRIERS THAT DIVIDE US.

> *But you will receive power when the Holy Spirit comes on you; and you will be my witnesses in Jerusalem, and in all Judea and Samaria, and to the ends of the earth. Acts 1:8*

Acts 1:8 commissions us to cross-cultural witness. Jesus says that his disciples will be empowered to be witnesses in Jerusalem, which is right where they were. Judea, the region occupied primarily by their fellow Jews, comes next. Beyond that, the disciples will be witnesses in Samaria. Samaria represents a cultural leap that requires overcoming a significant ethnic barrier. If we are to serve our marginalized neighbors, very often, it will mean reaching across ethnic, racial, and social barriers, too.

Even though Peter heard Jesus' commission, and even though Peter was empowered on the Day of Pentecost, Peter still didn't quite get it. Peter needed a vision from heaven before he was ready (Acts 10). What will get us ready?

We have already mentioned that sometimes followers of Jesus are intimidated by the thought of reaching out and up across social barriers. Sometimes, we can feel intimidated by the needs of people, as well. That's somewhat understandable if we are being exposed to needs we've never encountered before. We can easily feel inadequate for the task. Yet, Jesus said, "You will receive power." We are empowered by God to do what we can. We have also seen that God's love, working through us, is a major key to our outreach efforts. Our love can't be limited by ethnic or social differences.

Another attitude we have to be careful to avoid, however, is a feeling that we are reaching down in our outreach efforts.

How can we reach out across these barriers without a patronizing attitude? Sometimes, instead of feeling intimidated, Christians feel comfortable reaching out across the barriers because they feel they are reaching down. We shouldn't be intimidated by people that are of our own social standing. Neither should we feel superior to people that society at large has marginalized in any way. They are infinitely valuable to God and should be to us, too.

Paul says in 1 Corinthians 13 that we can do all kinds of ministry, including giving everything we have to the poor, but if we don't have love, we gain nothing (verse 3). **Paul then says in verse five that love does not dishonor others.** We want to make sure that in serving our marginalized neighbors, we love with honor.

Needs sometimes drive people to desperate measures and behavior judged as undesirable by society at large. I've seen people crowding, grasping, pushing at a food distribution. Sometimes people "abuse the system." For our witness to be effective, we have to be more concerned about loving people than protecting the system. Convoy of Hope refers to people who are being served through food distribution and community outreach as "guests of honor." God wants to honor and lift up marginalized people. We do, too.

## DAY 4 | JESUS LOVES MARGINALIZED PEOPLE THROUGH YOU.

At the beginning of his Gospel, John established the magnificent truth that God's Son, the One through whom all creation came into existence, became a human being and lived with us here on earth:

> *The Word became flesh and made his dwelling among us. We have seen his glory, the glory of the one and only Son, who came from the Father, full of grace and truth. John 1:14*

What a wonderful message! Jesus came in glory to bring us God's grace and truth. Jesus took on human flesh, something we call the Incarnation. And here's a truth that is especially meaningful to you and me as we serve God and our neighbors: Jesus is still taking on human flesh.

*Again Jesus said, "Peace be with you! As the Father has sent me, I am sending you." John 20:21*

Jesus sends us out into "incarnational ministry." One of the most prominent biblical metaphors for the church is the "body of Christ." We, as followers of Jesus Christ, form the body of Christ. We are Jesus' hands and feet. Together, we are doing the work of Jesus.

Since a body is made up of many different parts, the same is true of the body of Christ. That means that no matter what your gifts are, whether they are prominent or more hidden, you have an important part to play in God's work. Together, our gifts and efforts add up to something that glorifies God—which is why the world needs to see the good works we do together.

Some spiritual philosophies see this world as something bad and to be escaped. Jesus saw this world as something to be loved and redeemed, so much so that he became a part of it. While Jesus promises us eternal life, he demonstrated love and compassion for people while they are still in this material world. Jesus healed. Jesus fed the crowds when they were hungry. As Jesus' body, we continue Jesus' loving and redeeming ministry when we care for the needs of others.

FOR REFLECTION:

Ask God to help you see your community as something to be loved and redeemed. How does it feel to know that you are part of the body of Christ? What does it mean when we say that God loves the marginalized people of our communities through you?

## DAY 5 | WE OFFER GOOD NEWS TO THE POOR.

> *...and the scroll of the prophet Isaiah was handed to him. Unrolling it, he found the place where it is written: "The Spirit of the Lord is on me, because he has anointed me to proclaim good news to the poor. He has sent me to proclaim freedom for the prisoners and recovery of sight for the blind, to set the oppressed free, to proclaim the year of the Lord's favor." Luke 4:17-19*

Jesus came to fulfill the prophecy of Isaiah, as he indicates upon reading this passage from the scroll. Luke wants us to notice that high on Jesus' agenda for his ministry is "to proclaim good news to the poor."

Luke, probably more than any other Gospel, tends to emphasize Jesus' concern for people on the margins of society.

Both Luke and Matthew give us a set of Beatitudes, or blessings, spoken by Jesus. Of special interest for us with regard to our love and service to marginalized people is the difference between Matthew 5:3 and 6, and Luke 6:20-21a.

*Blessed are the poor in spirit, for theirs is the kingdom of heaven. Blessed are those who hunger and thirst for righteousness, for they will be filled. Matthew 5:3,6*

*Looking at his disciples, he said: "Blessed are you who are poor, for yours is the kingdom of God. Blessed are you who hunger now, for you will be satisfied." Luke 6:20-21a*

Notice that Matthew refers to "poor in spirit" while Luke simply says, "poor." Matthew also speaks of those "who hunger and thirst for righteousness" while Luke speaks blessing on "you who hunger now."

Which is correct? They both are, of course. What we need to know is that Luke, who was a physician, presents to us the mission of Jesus in a way that shows special concern for marginalized people with here-and-now needs. Spiritual needs are an important reality. Many of our everyday neighbors don't have major material needs, but we all have spiritual needs. Sometimes, however, people aren't ready to receive what they need for spiritual health because of overwhelming concerns of a more temporal nature. Jesus came to bring good news not only to the poor in spirit; he came to bring good news to the poor, whatever the nature of their poverty.

**FOR REFLECTION:**

What is the difference between good news for the poor and good news for the poor in spirit? Should we be concerned with both kinds of poverty? Why or why not?

*"Is not this the kind of fasting I have chosen: to loose the chains of injustice and untie the cords of the yoke, to set the oppressed free and break every yoke? Is it not to share your food with the hungry and to provide the poor wanderer with shelter— when you see the naked, to clothe him, and not to turn away from your own flesh and blood? Then your light will break forth like the dawn, and your healing will quickly appear; then your righteousness will go before you, and the glory of the LORD will be your rear guard. Then you will call, and the LORD will answer; you will cry for help, and he will say: Here am I." Isaiah 58:6-9*

## VIDEO NOTES

1. Why do you believe God has a heart for marginalized people?
2. How have you seen marginalized people lifted up by God in the past?
3. What is harder to address: people's physical needs or spiritual needs? Which needs, if any, are the most important? How might physical needs be connected with spiritual needs?
4. How can you continue to grow a heart that is more like God's heart for your marginalized neighbors?

## ACTION STEPS

1. Make an invitation to serve to your neighbor you identified from Week 2 if you haven't yet. See the script in the Appendix for help on what to say.
2. Pray daily for your friend to be blessed and respond to the invitation.
3. Commit to complete the five devotionals on the next pages before we gather for Week 5 of small group.

## PRAY TOGETHER

Pray as a whole group for our marginalized neighbors, in specific, those that you will be serving through your project.

# A HEART FOR GOD AND HIS FAMILY

## GROUP SESSION 5

This week you will grow stronger in your relationship with God and his family, the church.

### INTRODUCTION TO THIS WEEK'S DEVOTIONALS

This effort is not just about doing something for God and doing something for others. The truth is, you are really doing something for yourself because you will be growing in your relationship with God. You will grow in dependence on God as you step out of your comfort zone. As you depend on God more, you will learn more about his presence and power that are available to you in a measure that you have never experienced before.

*Loving each other is a part of our witness to the whole world! Jesus' prayer in John 17 affirms this: I have given them the glory that you gave me, that they may be one as we are one—I in them and you in me—so that they may be brought to complete unity. Then the world will know that you sent me and have loved them even as you have loved me. John 17:22–23*

Our unity or oneness is vital! Our unity lets the world know that the Father sent Jesus and has loved them. How do we show our unity to the world? It is being demonstrated to the world through our outreach to others as we in the church work together. People should see not only our love for God and our love for them but our love for each other in the church!

**How do we show our unity to the world? It is being demonstrated to the world through our outreach to others as we in the church work together. People should see not only our love for God and our love for them but our love for each other in the church!**

The church I pastor is very multiethnic. I think a multiethnic church, where possible, or a multiethnic fellowship of churches, represents the cure for much of the division our world faces. We show we are able to love each other in spite of potential barriers, such as race and politics. Jesus said this kind of unity would be a testimony of his love for lost humanity. But how are people going to witness this testimony we are giving? How are we going to display our unity? We do so powerfully every time we gather together for multiethnic worship. But what if people don't come to our worship gatherings?

When we go out and serve the community together, the people we serve will see our unity across potential social barriers. When we invite our everyday neighbors to serve with us, they will see it, too.

One goal of Convergence Evangelism is to welcome our world into the care of God's family. How can we do that if the members of God's family don't care for one another? This week we will grow in our love for God, in our dependence on God, and in our love for the neighbors who make up our church family. We will also grow in our understanding of God's plan for the Church.

## DAY 1 | YOU HAVE JESUS' AUTHORITY.

Let's revisit the Great Commission, which we mentioned in our introduction. We know that making disciples is something God expects of us as followers of Jesus. Does that sound like an expectation beyond your capacity? If so, let's talk about the ability to fulfill God's commands. God doesn't command us to do anything that he won't equip us to do. We see a couple of indications of this in Matthew 28. Let's look at these verses:

*Then Jesus came to them and said, "All authority in heaven and on earth has been given to me. Therefore go and make disciples of all nations, baptizing them in the name of the Father and of the Son and of the Holy Spirit, and teaching them to obey everything I have commanded you. And surely I am with you always, to the very end of the age." Matthew 28:18-20*

The heart of the Great Commission is this: "Make disciples," with baptizing and teaching describing how we make disciples. The power or ability to do so is offered in Jesus' statements about himself. First, Jesus says, "All authority in heaven and on earth has been given to me." When Jesus follows that up by telling us to make disciples, he's saying, in effect, "You are doing this under my authority, and you are doing this with my authority." Jesus has delegated authority to us as representatives of his kingdom. You have Jesus' authority to do everything pertaining to this outreach that God wants you to do. You are loving and serving your neighbors, bearing witness to God's goodness, using the authority of Jesus himself. That ought to help us with any anxiety we have about our mission!

Jesus also said after giving us the Great Commission: "And surely I am with you always, to the very end of the age." One thing this tells us, in case there was any doubt, is that the commission is not just for the disciples of Jesus' day. The Great Commission is for Jesus' disciples until the end of time.

Another vital meaning of Jesus' statement that he is always with us: We are not engaging in this endeavor alone. Jesus is with us in this! We not only have Jesus' authority; we have Jesus' presence with us.

We would do well to learn to rely on Jesus' presence for us to be effective and fruitful. A fantastic side benefit of being engaged in Jesus' commission: we learn more about Jesus' presence in our lives. Followers of Jesus who have known Jesus' presence in their lives, but who have not been very intentional about fulfilling the Great Commission have a fresh experience of Jesus awaiting them.

**FOR REFLECTION:**

What does it mean to you to know that Jesus has given you authority to do what he is asking you to do? What does it mean to know that you have Jesus' presence with you when you do what he is asking of you?

## DAY 2 | YOU WILL RECEIVE POWER FROM THE HOLY SPIRIT.

> *But you will receive power when the Holy Spirit comes on you; and you will be my witnesses in Jerusalem, and in all Judea and Samaria, and to the ends of the earth." Acts 1:8*

What enabled the original disciples to wait as they did, nine days after Jesus' promise in Acts 1:8, for the Spirit to be poured out on the Day of Pentecost? We can't know for sure, but I would venture to guess that one factor had to be that the disciples had received a command, the Great Commission, but they absolutely knew they could not fulfill it in their own strength. They were most likely well aware of their inabilities, especially considering how they had failed and scattered in connection with Jesus' crucifixion.

We also have a commission we can't fulfill in our own strength. We expect that people will respond to our invitations to serve with us, and we hope to worship with us, eventually. We are expecting that they will see our good works and begin to glorify God. We are expecting people to know God's love through our good deeds. If these are really going to happen, we are going to have to work in cooperation with God, with his strength, and with his spiritual authority. We have to have spiritual power.

Christians have varying views on experiences with the Holy Spirit, but we are all in agreement that the Spirit empowers and gifts us to live out God's purposes for our lives. We all agree that the Holy Spirit is one of the Trinity, and as such is as much infinite God as the Father and Son are. The fact that God is infinite hints to us that there is infinitely more of God to know and experience. It's not that God holds himself back from us when we receive Christ—he doesn't—but there is always more of God to get to know. God has more power available to you, too.

Two insights will help lead you into a deeper walk with God: 1) an awareness of our own inadequacies, and 2) an awareness that we can experience more of God's love and power than we have to this point. My genuine prayer is that these fresh insights lead all of us closer to God than we have ever been.

**FOR REFLECTION:**

In what ways are you inadequate for the task to which God has called you? Why is it okay to admit inadequacies? How does God make you adequate to the task? Ask God to fill you with his Spirit.

## DAY 3 | WHAT IS THE GREATEST COMMANDMENT?

We have recognized that without love, our serving gains us nothing. We have discussed the fact that the "royal law" of Scripture is to love our neighbor as ourselves. It's hard to imagine that any law or command in the Bible would be more important than that. Yet, Jesus says that there is one commandment of Scripture that tops it. Here's Jesus' response when he was asked by a religious leader what the greatest commandment was:

> *Jesus replied: "'Love the Lord your God with all your heart and with all your soul and with all your mind.' This is the first and greatest commandment." Matthew 22:37-38*

Jesus goes on to say that loving our neighbor as ourselves is like the first, but it's second to it. I wonder, can we adequately love others if we don't have the priority in order? I would imagine that we can be very loving individuals, but still have a greater capacity to love other people if we will put God first.

How can we put God first in our love lives? Is it by a force of will? Is it simply a decision we make? I'm all for choosing to love God, but I have to admit the inadequacy of my willpower alone. The best way for me to love God is to receive God's love for me. John tells us in 1 John 4:19,

> *We love because he first loved us. 1 John 4:19*

God's love has been extended to you through Jesus. While we were still far from God, Christ died for us to bring us life (Romans 5:8, 1 John 4:9). This is the true nature of love. God loves you as one of his own dear children, and the Holy Spirit has been given to you to make God's love a living reality for you (Romans 8:16). The more real God's love for you is, the more you will love him. And the more you love God, the more you will love your neighbor.

We can't adequately fulfill the Great Commission without attending to the Great Commandment: Love God with all that we are.

---

**FOR REFLECTION:**

How has God showed you his love for you? Why is it important to receive God's love? How does receiving God's love help you fulfill the Great Commandment? How does loving help you fulfill the Great Commission?

## DAY 4 | YOU HAVE DONE IT TO ME.

A restaurant near my home was obviously struggling, and you could see it in the owner's demeanor. The saddest part about the situation is that he was venting his frustration by speaking harshly to his daughter, who was working with him. I felt so badly for her. The food was really pretty good, but I never went back to that restaurant again. It wasn't because of the way they treated me. It was the way they treated their own family. Unfortunately, the restaurant has permanently closed.

We have noted that the second greatest commandment, the royal law, is to love our neighbor as we love ourselves. What probably goes unnoticed in a casual reading of many of the Bible verses on love is that they are about loving each other in God's family. Even 1 Corinthians 13, the "love chapter," which is so often read at weddings, is not really about love in marriage. The context is about love within the family of God, among the church's various members.

One of our favorite teachings of Jesus when it comes to serving people in need can be found in Matthew 25:

> Then the King will say to those on his right, 'Come, you who are blessed by my Father; take your inheritance, the kingdom prepared for you since the creation of the world. For I was hungry and you gave me something to eat, I was thirsty and you gave me something to drink, I was a stranger

*and you invited me in, I needed clothes and you clothed me, I was sick and you looked after me, I was in prison and you came to visit me.' Then the righteous will answer him, 'Lord, when did we see you hungry and feed you, or thirsty and give you something to drink? When did we see you a stranger and invite you in, or needing clothes and clothe you? When did we see you sick or in prison and go to visit you?' Matthew 25:34–39*

Notice Jesus emphasizes the importance of providing food, clothing, hospitality, something to drink, and care for the sick or imprisoned. The real stunner in this story is verse 40, a surprise even to the ones Jesus is welcoming into his kingdom:

*The King will reply, 'Truly I tell you, whatever you did for one of the least of these brothers and sisters of mine, you did for me.' Matthew 25:40*

That's so powerful: when we serve "the least of these," we have served Jesus himself. But, here's another shocker for many of us who are already familiar with this verse: When Jesus refers to the least of his brothers and sisters, he wasn't talking about loving the poor of the world. He was talking about loving others within the body of Christ. Everywhere else in Scripture that Jesus refers to "brothers and sisters," he is referring specifically to his followers, people who have chosen to be his disciples. What does this mean for us? It means that if we want to love and serve Jesus, we are to love and serve his church.

I'm not suggesting that we forget about serving the poor outside the church. The Bible clearly teaches us to do that—just not in Matthew 25! We have seen in week four that we are indeed called to love and serve people outside the church. However, for us to share love with people outside the church, we have to start with loving one another in the church. The Bible says,

> *Therefore, as we have opportunity, let us do good to all people, especially to those who belong to the family of believers. Galatians 6:10*

We do good to all people, but we start in the church.

**FOR REFLECTION:**

In what ways are you challenged by the Bible's teaching that loving people in need starts in the family of believers? How will loving our brothers and sisters in Christ enhance our ability to do good to all people?

## DAY 5 | OUR UNITY IS A POWERFUL WITNESS FOR JESUS.

In Jesus' high priestly prayer, he prays for his followers:

> *I in them and you in me—so that they may be brought to complete unity. Then the world will know that you sent me and have loved them even as you have loved me. John 17:23*

My wife and I once visited a church where we noticed a certain trend: Many of the men in the church had the same haircut as the pastor! There's nothing wrong with that, but it's important to know that we aren't unified as the church because we all think, act, dress, vote, and get our hair cut the same way. We aren't unified by our preferences for certain music styles. We are unified around Jesus, our love for him, and our love for his family, the church. In a world that is racked by chaos and division, our unity across all sorts of ethnic and social barriers sends a powerful message. Our love for each other within the church is God's solution for mending a world broken by ethnic and political strife.

Jesus tells us in John 17:23 that one of the most effective ways to convey God's love to a lost and hurting world is to demonstrate our love for one another in the church. We touched on this in week 3. It's important to look at this verse again in the context of our own growth in love for God and for his family.

The unity Jesus is speaking of is not just an organizational unity, but one centered on our receiving the love of God and then extending that love to one another.

The question remains for us to ask ourselves: How will our neighbors get an opportunity to see our amazing, God-given unity if they don't attend a worship service? The answer is that they will get a glimpse of our unity when they are served by us or when they serve with us. Keep in mind that some people are ready to serve with us before they are ready to worship with us.

The outreach we are doing through this endeavor is itself a powerful witness, too. People will see God's light through our good works, and they will glorify our Father in heaven (Matthew 5:16). We should believe that what Jesus says about that is true. We should also firmly believe Jesus' words in John 17:23, where Jesus prays that we would be brought to complete unity with this result:

> *Then the world will know that you sent me and have loved them even as you have loved me. John 17:23b*

Our unity doesn't just tell the world that we love each other in the family of God. Our unity tells the world that God loves us, and if God loves us, he loves them, too.

Several members of our church would often go to a local restaurant where we got to know the owner, who was not a follower of Jesus. She was, however, very curious about God and our faith, and we had many opportunities for conversations about Christ. One day a member of our church was talking to the owner, and it became clear to the owner that this customer attended the same church as the rest of us. When that fact dawned on the owner, she exclaimed, "You go to the church where God loves everybody!" That's exactly the message we want to convey through our love for our neighbors and our love for one another.

With Convergence Evangelism, we see a powerful convergence occurring when we put the principles of John 17:23 into action.

1. Serving with our church family demonstrates Jesus' love for the world through our acts of kindness (Mt. 5:16, 1 Peter 2:12).

2. Serving with our church family demonstrates Jesus' love for the world through our love for one another (the way we treat our brothers and sisters during our service project) (John 17:23).

3. People see the good works of the family of God and glorify our Father in heaven (Matthew 5:16).

We have looked at the incarnational ministry. Our service to the community as a church speaks volumes to the community at large – not just the neighbors you invite to serve with you.

FOR REFLECTION:

Why do you think God chose to bear witness to the world by means of the unity of the family of God? Why would someone who is not a follower of Jesus see a unified church and then come to the conclusion that God loves the world? Pray that our neighbors, including the people we are inviting to serve with us, see our unity and as a result, see God's love.

## 🏠 WEEK 5 | SMALL GROUP

### VIDEO NOTES

### QUESTIONS FOR DISCUSSION

1. Why is the local church important in God's plan?
2. Why is unity vital? What is the connection between our unity as followers of Christ and our witness to our world?
3. If people don't attend our worship services, how can they see the church's unity? How can inviting someone to serve with us help them see our unity?
4. Do these concepts challenge any of your previous mindsets or beliefs?
5. What do you see as your personal role in God's plan for the local church? How can we grow in love for one another as the family of God?

## ACTION STEPS

1. Make an invitation to serve to your neighbor you identified from Week 2 if you haven't yet. See the script in the Appendix for help on what to say.
2. Follow up on the invitation if you're still waiting for a response.
3. Pray daily for your friend to be blessed and respond to the invitation.
4. Commit to complete the five devotionals on the next pages before we gather for Week 6 of small group.

## PRAY TOGETHER

This week, in groups of 3, pray for those who you are inviting to serve with you as well as your project.

# YOUR CALL TO ACTION AND PRAYER

## GROUP SESSION 6

This week you will grow in your faith that God is hearing and answering your prayers on behalf of the people we are called to reach.

### INTRODUCTION TO THIS WEEK'S DEVOTIONALS

This is an exciting week! Your Day of Service, or your service project, will take place this week if you are following the plan. You have grown in your desire to fulfill God's call on your own life, which includes the good works he has prepared in advance for you to do. You are expecting God to receive glory through our efforts together. You know that your everyday neighbors are motivated to live lives of significance, and you can help them take steps toward God's plans for them. God has given you a heart to reach out to, and include in your circle of love, the people who too often are marginalized by society. Perhaps most importantly, you are growing in the knowledge of God and in your relationship with his family.

Convergence Evangelism is, after all, a highly spiritual endeavor. Our service projects and our working together require a lot of organization and effort, but the impact on our world, our churches, and our own lives will be minimal if we don't lean on the Lord.

This week, we want to redouble our prayer efforts. We are asking God to help us to see the opportunities he is putting before us. We want to see our everyday and marginalized neighbors the way God sees them. Our goal is that people see the benevolent reign of God, that they truly sense the love of God through us, and that a bit more of God's will be done on earth. We want to grow in our faith that God will do miracles in our hearts and lives. Jesus encourages us to pray such things with boldness, so we will be getting a fresh look at some of the petitions of the Lord's Prayer. It's powerful!

If you are a seasoned prayer warrior, you probably know that many of us praying in unity will be powerful. If you aren't confident about God hearing and answering your prayers, you are in for a

> Convergence evangelism is, after all, a highly spiritual endeavor.

wonderful spiritual awakening. Whether in a big or small way, God is going to come through in response to your prayers. We are also going to help with some God-given patterns of prayer that will serve you well not just for this project, but for the rest of your walk with Jesus.

Prayer works. A while back, I was needing to drive to an important meeting, but had misplaced my car keys. As the time to leave got closer, I became increasingly frustrated. As I was frantically looking all over the house and asking my family if they had seen my keys, my father-in-law asked me, "Well, did you pray about it?" I couldn't believe he would have the nerve to ask me, a pastor, if I had prayed about something. Don't pastors pray about everything? I guess not, because the truth is, I hadn't prayed. So I stopped, said a little prayer asking God to guide me, immediately had a thought as to the location, and when I looked, there were the keys. If God can answer a prayer concerning lost keys, he will answer our prayers concerning people who might be lost when it comes to having a personal relationship with God.

We can't just talk about it. We have to pray about it.

NOTE: Your day of service will possibly take place during this week. If the day of service occurs before Group Session 6, you are still encouraged to do the devotionals and come together for the group session after your day of service. The prayer principles of this week are important for your ongoing walk with God.

*Don't you have a saying, 'It's still four months until harvest'? I tell you, open your eyes and look at the fields! They are ripe for harvest. John 4:35*

"People aren't interested in God." I've heard this and similar sayings ever since I've been a follower of Christ. Sure, we know that an increasing number of people in the United States claim no religious affiliation. But, does that mean people are not interested in God? I don't think so. For one, we see by lots of measures that people frequently think about God. We see a surge of interest in prayer during times of crisis, for example. The number one indicator of people's readiness to connect with God, however, is not from recent surveys; it's from the mouth of Jesus: "I tell you, open your eyes and look at the fields! They are ripe for harvest."

We might feel as though no one is ready for our witness, whether by words or by deeds. We may even know some people who give lots of evidence that they're closed to our witness. It seems to me, though, that the main problem with feeling that people aren't ready is that feelings don't always tell the truth. When we are uncomfortable about taking certain actions, it's easy to make our discomfort bigger than reality. When it comes to our witness, we need God's perspective. That's why Jesus says, "Open your eyes and look at the fields!"

Ask God to give you his perspective on the people we will be serving in our outreach. Ask for God's perspective on the people we are inviting to serve with us—people who do not yet know Jesus, who are not yet ready to worship with us, perhaps. If they are serving with us, they are certainly ready to see our good works and move one step closer to glorifying our Father. The fields are ripe for harvest. Another point Jesus makes elsewhere, in Luke 10, about the harvest: It's not only ripe, but it's also plentiful.

> He told them, "The harvest is plentiful, but the workers are few. Ask the Lord of the harvest, therefore, to send out workers into his harvest field."
> Luke 10:2

Along with making such a positive statement about the harvest, Jesus identifies a problem: not enough workers! Convergence Evangelism doesn't represent the totality of evangelism and making disciples. It does, however, bring together a number of powerful spiritual dynamics to make an impact for God's glory:

1. People see our good deeds and glorify our Father in heaven.
2. People see our unity and receive a witness of God's love for people.
3. People who serve alongside us begin to connect with their God-given purpose.

Another powerful dynamic is that it begins to mobilize more workers for God's harvest. Convergence Evangelism helps many of us as followers of Jesus to begin to realize that we can make a real difference in other people's lives. We can offer a testimony through our deeds. We can be prepared to give a reason for the hope we have.

Let's pray! Let's pray that we will open our eyes and see the opportunities that are there. Let's pray for more and more workers in God's harvest field. Let's pray that God be glorified through his church and through our lives like we would never have dreamed.

**FOR REFLECTION:**

Ask God to send more workers for the harvest of people he wants to bring into relationship with himself. Ask God to help you and other workers see how ready people are to receive the Good News of Jesus.

You are probably stepping out of your comfort zone by participating in outreach and by inviting an everyday neighbor to serve with you. You are being asked to do something that might be out of the norm for you. You are engaging in the act of witnessing to your marginalized neighbors and your everyday neighbors, sending a message of God's love. If it feels a little uncomfortable, then the response of the church in Acts 4 might be encouraging to you.

The followers of Jesus in Acts 4 had begun to experience threats in relation to their witness. They were warned not even to speak of Jesus. Their response was to pray. In their prayer, they refer to Scripture and declare to God who he is, what he has promised and planned, and what he has done. On that foundation, they then make a request for themselves.

> *Now, Lord, consider their threats and enable your servants to speak your word with great boldness.*
> *Acts 4:29*

Amazingly, they express more concern about their mission than about their own safety! They were willing to do what they had to do, but they knew they needed God's help to do it. They needed boldness that only God can give. We may face different challenges to our witness, but we also need boldness for our own circumstances. God will give you that boldness if you ask him.

Here's another thing the church prayed for in Acts 4: "Stretch out your hand to heal and perform signs and wonders through the name of your holy servant Jesus" (Acts 4:30).

Jesus' followers not only asked for boldness to do their part; they asked for God to do his part, too. We should ask the same: "God, do miracles that only you can do." God didn't let the early church down. In our time, in our situation, God will do his part, too. You can count on that. If you do your part, God will do his and bring healing. He will heal hurting communities, broken spirits, wounded souls. You may see God bring about healings that go beyond your expectations.

So, are you stepping out of your comfort zone? Good! That's all the more reason to pray. Let's pray for the boldness to do our part. Let's pray for God to do his part.

**FOR REFLECTION:**
Pray for the person you have invited to follow through on their commitment to serve with you. Pray for them to have their spiritual eyes open to what God wants them to see. Pray that they will experience a witness of God's love for them.

Since we're devoting emphasis to prayer this week, we should take a look at the pattern of prayer that Jesus gave us in Matthew 6. It is, after all, a part of the sermon in which we find our primary verse for Convergence Evangelism, Matthew 5:16:

> *In the same way, let your light shine before others, that they may see your good deeds and glorify your Father in heaven.*

What is the end result of letting our good deeds be seen by others? People will glorify our Father in heaven.

In the Lord's Prayer, which Jesus gave us as a pattern for prayer, we find what should be our priorities in prayer. Jesus didn't give us the Lord's Prayer just to recite; he gave it to us as a pattern to guide our heart's desires as expressed through prayer. What's our top priority in prayer? "Our Father in heaven, hallowed be your name" (Matthew 6:9). God's name represents who God is. For God's name to be hallowed, people must see him and acknowledge him for who he is. That is, God will be glorified.

Our desire is to see God glorified, not just in the church, but throughout the world, including our own little part of the world. The goal for our efforts in loving and serving our neighbors is for God to be glorified. In our praying and in our outreach, the result we want to see is that people honor and glorify God for who he is.

It's great that the names of our churches become known in our communities. I love seeing volunteers serving in our communities while wearing t-shirts with church names on them. That way, the people we serve or who are serving with us know that they are witnessing the family of God at work. Knowing our church names will help people know where they can turn to grow closer to God. Our ultimate goal, however, is for the name of God to be hallowed and glorified. Let's pray for that to happen.

**FOR REFLECTION:**

Is glorifying God your primary goal? Ask him to help you make it your priority. Pray that God would be glorified through our churches and our service projects.

We have seen in our study that the early church's priority was to continue their mission as Jesus' witnesses to their world. We've also seen that the priority Jesus gave us, both for our good deeds and for our prayers, is that God be glorified. The next priority Jesus gives us in the Lord's Prayer is revolutionary:

> *Your kingdom come, your will be done, on earth as it is in heaven. Matthew 6:10*

Jesus is not saying here we should pray to go to heaven. He's saying we should pray that the earth becomes more like heaven. We should pray for God to rule and reign here on this earth. This is revolutionary because the hurt, pain, and evil we see in the world represent the status quo for far too many people. While we know that ultimately God is sovereign over all the earth, we have evidence that another kingdom, a dark kingdom, holds too much sway. The devil is defeated, but he is still active. The good news is that Jesus came to destroy the work of the devil and to establish God's benevolent rule.

We want to see God set wrong things right. When you pray for this and then really live for this, God is going to use you to do so through your service. We are resisting the status quo that would see this world locked in decay and darkness. When we pray and do good, when we live in the love and unity only God can bring, when we bear witness to the Good News, we are continuing the mission of Jesus.

When God's kingdom comes, it's not just a matter of overthrowing systems. God's kingdom also comes when an individual acknowledges and glorifies God as King. The kingdom of God is not a place or a political system; the kingdom is anywhere the King rules, including a human heart. We have a strong expectation that when people see your good works, they are moved closer to acknowledging God as the King of their hearts.

## FOR REFLECTION:

What does it mean to let God be the King of your heart? Ask God to help the person you invited to serve with you open their heart to God's kingship. What evidences of the rule of God to you expect to see in your community? Pray for those things to happen.

We've recognized that our activity, apart from prayer, will produce ineffective results. The fruit from all our hard work and organization will be minimal without prayer and trust that God will be at work. But we can't forget that God will be working through people, through us. God will shine his light on the people we are loving and serving, but he will be doing so through you. We have to apply ourselves to the task at hand.

In a verse that applies to God's people after the coming of our Redeemer, the Bible says,

> *Arise, shine, for your light has come, and the glory of the Lord rises upon you. Isaiah 60:1*

In some ways, this is quite simple: Just rise up and shine because God is already at work shining on you. As we saw in week one, Jesus declares that you are the salt of the earth; you are the light of the world (Matthew 5:13-14). As a follower of Jesus, you have a new identity (2 Corinthians 5:17), so a good word for engaging in your project is, "You do you."

Don't be anxious. Don't pressure yourself to have to perform in front of other church members, with friends or family serving with you, or with the people, we are serving. You are salt; you are light. Accept your identity in Christ. Just be what and who you are in Christ. Remember this word of encouragement and its accompanying promise:

> *Do not be anxious about anything, but in every situation, by prayer and petition, with thanksgiving, present your requests to God. And the peace of God, which transcends all understanding, will guard your hearts and your minds in Christ Jesus. Philippians 4:6–7*

Arise, shine, for your light has come.

**FOR REFLECTION:**

What anxieties do you need to present to God? Take time right now to give these things over to him. Thank God for taking these things, and replacing your anxiety with his peace.

## VIDEO NOTES

## QUESTIONS FOR DISCUSSION

1. What insights on prayer have you gained this past week? How has God already been working in you during this whole process?
2. What is the relationship between our prayers and our action? Are they mutually exclusive? Are prayer and action interdependent? Why or why not?
3. How has prayer changed you in the past? Have you ever committed to pray for something regularly? If so, what happened?
4. Has God ever spoken to you through prayer? If so, what did He say?

## ACTION STEPS

1. Remind the person you have invited of the service project. Let them know that you appreciate their willingness to serve with you.
2. Plan to pick them up, or meet them at a specific time and place. Maybe you can even plan to take them to lunch after you serve together!

## PRAY IN UNISON

Heavenly Father, thank you for including each of us in your plan. We embrace your will for our lives. We receive your love and your empowerment. Fill us afresh with your Holy Spirit. Help us grow in our love for You. Help us to love each other within your family. Help us to love our neighbors as we love ourselves. May our love and our acts of service bring glory to You. In Jesus' name, Amen.

**Script:**

I know you (like to volunteer, love others so well, enjoying giving back to the community) and I was hoping you'd consider serving alongside me at my church's Big Day of Hope. I'll be serving at [name specific project]. Do you think you'd like to volunteer with me?

**Sample Invite Card:**

FRONT

**DAY OF HOPE**
**OCTOBER 23, 2021**

BACK (Writable Material)

# WOULD YOU SERVE WITH ME?

## I'M SERVING AT PROJECT_____

Get all the information and sign
up at **DAYOFHOPE.CARE**

You can download an adaptable version of this checklist at inviteyourneighbor.com.

## Checklist for Participating Churches: Invite Your Neighbor to Serve

Some of our neighbors are ready to serve with us before they're ready to worship with us.

Goal: Reach our neighbors who need our service; reach our neighbors who will serve with us.

### Spring:
- ❏ Select church coordinator
- ❏ Select church prayer representative
- ❏ Select small groups coordinator
- ❏ Attend pastor and leader training on _____ (date).
- ❏ Attend project coordinator meeting on _____ (date).
- ❏ Order curriculum for small groups

### Nine to ten weeks out:
- ❏ Enlist key leaders who will be inviting others to serve with them
- ❏ Explain to each of them Invite Your Neighbor to Serve
- ❏ Send each of them a thank you email and a confirmation
- ❏ Begin small groups signups

### Eight weeks out:
- ❏ Form your church prayer team for the outreach
- ❏ Train church prayer team in prayer for the outreach, the neighbors we will invite to serve with us, and people being served

- ❏ Get graphics ready for bulletin board and website
- ❏ Get invitation cards ready
- ❏ Get Invite Your Neighbor to Serve prayer/commitment cards ready (members will put names of their neighbor on the card)
- ❏ Use social media strategically
- ❏ Order T-shirts for your church volunteers (use your church's name and logo, or event name and logo)
- ❏ Continue small groups signups

### Seven weeks out:
- ❏ Introduce Converge Day and the call to serve to your church
- ❏ Introduce the idea of Invite Your Neighbor to Serve
- ❏ Distribute prayer/commitment cards to each church attendee
- ❏ Distribute invite cards to each attendee
- ❏ Begin online project signups using project menu
- ❏ Let the church know of the Converge Day website
- ❏ Continue small groups signups

### Six weeks out:
- ❏ One or a few key leaders announce their "neighbor" (who they are inviting to serve with them)
- ❏ Distribute prayer/commitment cards to each church attendee
- ❏ Distribute invite cards to each attendee
- ❏ Continue online project sign-ups using project menu (to be provided)
- ❏ Put completed prayer cards on the bulletin board and put digital representations on the website
- ❏ Begin Converge small groups

### Five weeks out:

- ❏ Other leaders announce their "One"
- ❏ Distribute prayer/commitment cards to each church attendee
- ❏ Distribute invite cards to each attendee
- ❏ Continue online project sign-ups using project menu (to be provided)
- ❏ Put completed cards on the bulletin board and put digital representations on the website

### Four weeks out:

- ❏ Members turn in the names of their "One"
- ❏ Distribute prayer/commitment cards to each church attendee
- ❏ Distribute invite cards to each attendee
- ❏ Continue project sign-ups using project menu (to be provided)
- ❏ Preach first sermon: having a heart to serve the community

### Three weeks out:

- ❏ Members turn in the names of their "One"
- ❏ Distribute prayer/commitment cards to each church attendee
- ❏ Distribute invite cards to each attendee
- ❏ Continue project sign-ups using project menu (to be provided)
- ❏ Preach second sermon: having a heart to reach your own neighbors (The Great Commission)

### Two weeks out:

- ❏ Members turn in the names of their "One"
- ❏ Distribute prayer/commitment cards to each church attendee
- ❏ Distribute invite cards to each attendee
- ❏ Continue project sign-ups using project menu (to be provided)

- ❏ Preach third sermon: letting your light shine so that those who see your good works (not just those who benefit from them) are more likely to glorify God (Matthew 5:16)

## Sunday before event:
- ❏ Members turn in the names of their invited neighbor
- ❏ Distribute prayer/commitment cards to each church attendee
- ❏ Distribute invite cards to each attendee
- ❏ Continue project sign-ups using project menu (to be provided)
- ❏ Preach fourth sermon: having a heart for community transformation

## Day of Event:
- ❏ Converge Day outreach
- ❏ Follow up with a thank you email to people from your church
- ❏ Follow up with a thank you to the "Ones" invited to serve by your church people
- ❏ Invite your "Ones" to worship with you

## Serve and Invite: Keep it Simple.

**Engaging Your Church People: Keep your asks simple.**
There are a lot of moving parts to a day of service with multiple projects. Our rationale for our actions, particularly that some of our near neighbors are ready to serve with us before they are ready to worship with us, must be made clear and kept in focus. The planning of projects, the publicity necessary, and the actual mobilization of the volunteers add a degree of complexity for the church leadership. Church leadership can't, however, allow any complexity of their task to be conveyed to the people in the church as a whole. **Once small groups being, we are simply making two asks of the people: find a place to serve, and invite someone to serve with you. That's it.**

Here's an example of our message, to be used by pastors, small group leaders, and others:

"You have forty projects from which to choose. We are simply asking you to do this: sign up for a project where you will serve, and invite someone to serve with you. Remember: some of your friends, family, coworkers, and classmates will be ready to serve with your before they are ready to worship with you."

We hand out a card to each individual in church that encourages these two commitments, serving and inviting. On one side of the card can be the church logo, or the branding for the day of service, the date of the project, and the web address for online signups. On the other side of the card there are two statements:

I will sign up to serve in project number _____. (Sign up at church website.)

I will invite _____ to serve with me.

We actually give each individual two of these cards, one to keep as a reminder to serve and invite, and the other to turn in so that the prayer team can pray for the invitees. Note: this is not a signup card; this is simply a commitment and reminder card. Of course, it could be turned into a signup card by adding a place to put the church person's name. The main point is that you are making it clear that you are only asking for two things, for church attendees to serve and for them to invite someone to serve with them.

**Keep it unintimidating.** We are not asking people to invite as many as they possibly can. Inviting too many people to serve with us could prevent our being as relational as we need to be with our neighbors. We are attempting to mobilize everyone in our churches to participate, and for everyone to invite just one. If someone invites more than one, of course that's allowed. What we encourage and celebrate, however, is not that someone has invited a large number to serve with them. What we celebrate is that everyone participated and invited. The goal is 100 percent participation.

We want all of our church attendees to participate in demonstrating the love of God through serving and inviting someone to serve.

**What are we celebrating?** We are not just celebrating numbers of people serving. We are celebrating that so many people are demonstrating the love of God. We are not providing ourselves reasons to boast about what we have done. We are providing ourselves reasons to boast about what God has done, and he has used us to demonstrate his love to people. He's demonstrated his love to our near neighbors as they saw the light of God at work in us, and he's demonstrated his love to our marginal neighbors as we glorified God with our serving. A focus on loving our neighbors and glorifying God is worth celebrating!

**How to invite an everyday neighbor to serve with you.** Here's a sample script that everyone can adapt to invite friends, family, coworkers, classmates, and others to serve with us:

> On (date) our church will be conducting service projects all around the community. I'm going to be (name task, such as "painting," "serving lunches to the homeless," etc.) at (location) at (time). We've been asked to invite a friend to serve with us. Would you join me in serving?

**What kinds of service projects should you conduct?**
Practically anything you do to serve the needs of your community will work, but again, keep it simple. Some of the best things you can do are service projects that assist ministries, organizations, and agencies that are already doing work in the community. One of my favorites is to do facilities projects at a public school in a very challenged school district. We have distributed food, coats, and clothing to the homeless, done maintenance for a city park, offered medical screenings, and many other activities.

A few principles to keep in mind:

- Be specific about the project
- Make a list of resources (tools, paint, etc.) that are needed.
- Provide the resources that are needed. Some agencies lack the funds to do what the project seeks to do. We don't want to be a burden in our attempt to help.
- Know how many volunteers can be adequately put to work. It is disheartening for volunteers to show up to serve and have nothing to do.
- Set a limited time for how long you will serve. A couple of hours for each team is usually a good guide.
- Be clear about the time and location volunteers are expected to show up.
- Begin your serve time with a brief, unintimidating prayer together. Our guest volunteers know they are participating in a church project and won't be offended.

You can download an adaptable version of this project proposal at inviteyourneighbor.com.

**Project Contact Person:**

**Goal:** Develop relationships where our church can bless and support the ongoing work of community organizations, agencies, and ministries.

**Provide the following project details:**

Location where we can serve (address/building):
_____
_____

Time of the event?
Begin: _____ AM / PM
End: _____ AM / PM

Scope of work (what will we accomplish on the Day of Hope at this location)?
_____
_____

Estimated # of Volunteers needed:
minimum: _____
maximum: _____

Can children participate? If Yes, Ages: _____

Project leader: _____
E-mail: _____
Deadline for submitting proposal: _____(date)

**Script to solicit interest from an organization/leader for hosting a serve team:**

We are planning to mobilize hundreds of people from Victory Church to serve on Saturday March 28th. Is there something that we can help with/donate/or provide volunteers for on that day that will benefit your organization?

| # | Project | | Name | Phone # |
|---|---------|---|------|---------|
| | | Project Leader | | |
| | | Assistant Leader | | |
| | | Workflow Manager | | |
| | | Care Manager | | |
| | | Lunch pick-up (@ Victory Church) | | |

## Supplies

| **Your team is Bringing:** Items you would ask your volunteers to bring after they sign-up (examples: work gloves, paint brushes, rakes, etc...) | **Church Buying:** What you need to complete the job that you cannot borrow from Victory or have volunteers bring (examples: paint, rollers, flowers, etc...) | **Asking for donation:** What we can ask corporations for donations for (examples: coats for coat drive, water, cleaning supplies, etc...) | **Borrowing from Church:** If we already have something in excess you can use (example: tables, vacuum, dropcloths, coolers, etc...) |
|---|---|---|---|
| | | | |
| | | | |
| | | | |
| | | | |
| | | | |
| | | | |
| | | | |
| | | | |
| | | | |
| | | | |

### Lunch need?

| | Does your team or do the people you are serving need lunch? |
|---|---|
| Yes | |
| No | |
| # needed | Quanity of bagged lunches that your site will need. |

**Lunches for each site will be picked up at Victory Church, 2650 Audubon Rd, Audubon between 11AM-noon on 9/28. Project manager will arrange for pick-up**

# APPENDIX 5: OTHER ADAPTABLE DOCUMENTS AVAILABLE

Here are some other practical, usable documents you can download to plan and execute your day of service at inviteyourneighbor.com.

- Small Group Leader Guide
- Project Planning Supply Spreadsheet
- Project Leader Guidelines
- Prayer Team Outline
- Communication Plan with Sample Emails